Daniel Biella

Replication of Classical Psychological Experiments in Virtual Environments

Von der Fakultät für Ingenieurwissenschaften der Universität Duisburg-Essen
zur Erlangung des akademischen Grades eines Doktors der Naturwissenschaften
(Dr. rer. nat.) genehmigte Dissertation.

Referent: Prof. Dr. W. Luther
Koreferent: Prof. Dr. M. Hemmje
Tag der mündlichen Prüfung: 12.10.2006

Bibliografische Information der Deutschen Nationalbibliothek

Die Deutsche Nationalbibliothek verzeichnet diese Publikation in der
Deutschen Nationalbibliografie; detaillierte bibliografische Daten sind
im Internet über http://dnb.d-nb.de abrufbar.

ISBN 3-8325-1440-6
ISBN13 978-3-8325-1440-2

Logos Verlag Berlin
Comeniushof, Gubener Str. 47,
10243 Berlin
Tel.: +49 030 42 85 10 90
Fax: +49 030 42 85 10 92
INTERNET: http://www.logos-verlag.de

Acknowledgements

I would like to express my gratitude toward my advisor, Prof. Dr. Wolfram Luther, who gave me the opportunity to work in his research group. He provided an exciting working environment with many opportunities to develop new ideas, work on promising applications and meet interesting people. I would also like to thank Prof. Dr. Matthias Hemmje for accepting the task of being the second reviewer of this thesis.

Additionally, I would like to thank Prof. Dr. H.-Peter Musahl, Prof. em. Dr. Gerd Mietzel, Lothar Wormuth, and Frank Bick for the fruitful discussions about the psychology-related aspects.

I would also like to thank all my colleagues who turned these years at the Institute of Informatics and Interactive Systems (IIIS) into a pleasant time.

Last but not least, I would like to thank my parents Klaus and Ursula Biella, my family, and my friends for their patience and support.

Contents

Chapter 1

Introduction

1.1 Scope of the work

This thesis was motivated by an interdisciplinary research project[1], initiated by the University of Duisburg-Essen, for the promotion of research foci ("Hochschulinternes Programm zur Förderung von Schwerpunktthemen der Forschung"). The project, mentored by Prof. Dr. Friedrich Wilkening (Psychological Institute, University of Zurich), was intended to demonstrate the historical impact of classical psychological experiments by the replication of those, which had a substantial influence on the development of psychology as a science and to highlight the central scientific methodology of experimentation in social science.

Right from its beginning as a new subject at universities - for example, the foundation of the "Institute for Experimental Psychology" at the University of Leipzig by W. Wundt in 1879 - psychology was an experimental science. In spite of the ups and downs in the history of psychology during the first half of the last century, nowadays the international orientation of psychology is toward the experimental paradigm. In fact, on September 17, 1982, the International Union of Psychological Science (IUPsyS) became the nineteenth full member of the International Council for Science (ICSU).

Five historical key experiments, first proposed by Skinner, Ebbinghaus, Sperling, Tolman, and Duncker, have been selected to illustrate this development. These experiments represent a historical tour through experimental psychology in two respects: The reconstructed 3D key experiments are arranged sequentially according to the historical scientific progress of research on learning and cognition. Furthermore, preceding or succeeding experiments in the historical context of a reconstructed key experiment can optionally be added and are chronologically arranged to underline the conceptual development of an experimental setup or methodology.

---

[1]The project was a cooperation between the department of computer science (Prof. Dr. W. Luther) and the department of psychology (Prof. Dr. H.-P. Musahl, Prof. em. Dr. G. Mietzel).

When creating virtual environments it is important to consider the specific context, that is, environmental and technical conditions, way of thinking, Zeitgeist, available methods of data analysis, approach and significance of a problem against the background of what was known at that time. Students as well as lecturers and teachers (referred to collectively in the following as users) have to accept that scientific progress means excluding false ideas, answers and hypotheses step by step. Users are thus enabled to accept that and discuss how misinterpretations arise. They learn to comprehend the limitations of the replication of given experiments through real examples and to estimate the validity of the results.

Although psychology, as a subject, is integrated in both school and university education plans and contributes its scientific results to many other areas, including sports, languages, and social sciences, there are relatively few interactive web-based implementations with psychology-related content. According to Stangl this has two reasons [Sta00]: On the one hand, many experts in psychology and education have insufficient technical expertise for the implementation of such systems. On the other hand, many standard software systems are not suited for the reproduction of complex human action. Hence, existing solutions are mainly limited to statistical aspects of psychology or to text databases. Web sites dedicated to the history of psychology are often limited to chronological representation of content that exists mainly in text-based form.

According to Mietzel [Mie01b], experts in educational psychology have, for a long time, pointed at shortcomings in the presentation of information that leave learners in a passive role. The online supplement [Mie01a] of the introductory psychological course book "Wege in die Psychologie" [Mie98] represents one of the few existing solutions in the field of psychology following the concept of a constructivist learning environment. The system has received positive feedback over the recent years and its web access statistics show page hits of up to 10000 hits/month [BLM+03a], which underlines the user's demand for such systems. The online supplement uses text-based information, images, and interactive animations. However, 3D virtual environments or complex simulation-driven models are not included.

In their article "The LeMO Project - Development of an Internet Multimedia Information System of 20th Century German History: Aims and Results" [ASRN01], Asmuss et al. discuss a virtual 3D museum implementation in VRML with hyperlinked 2D multimedia documents. By the end of 2000, LeMO contained some 31 3D environments and over 5000 multimedia web pages covering various periods, topics, chronicles, and biographies from German history. The LeMO project has shown the technical feasibility of deploying a web-based virtual environment with a large multimedia content base. The optional VRML-based 3D visualization has been designed with the intention to give each historical period a characteristic representation by visualizing metaphors as 3D environments and stresses the importance of metaphorical design considerations in 3D visualization.

Metaphorical design is discussed in a paper entitled "Exploiting the Potential of 3D Navigable Virtual Exhibition Spaces" by C. Cerulli [Cer99], in which the author is concerned with the definition of the historical and cultural context in which the development of virtual exhibition space needs to be placed. Cerulli proposes a survey throughout the years from the sixteenth century's galleries to contemporary web-based virtual galleries, where the exhibition space could be a text-based environment, a 2D graphical interface, or a 3D model accessible through the Internet and visualized by digital images, videos, 3D computer models, and virtual sculptures. Important analogies and differences between real and virtual museums are developed.

A more theoretical approach of state-of-the-art virtual museums is given in the article "Toward the Synchronized Experiences between Real and Virtual Museum" by Y.-M. Kwon *et al.* [KHL+03]. The authors propose a model of a virtual museum by defining real and virtual museum services, grouping them in the three logical layers *inspection*, *research and communication*, and *documentation and storage*, and synchronizing both real and virtual museum services.

One of the few interactive psychological virtual experiments based on a non-deterministic behavior simulation model is described in the article "Sniffy, the virtual rat: Simulated operant conditioning" by J. Graham, T. Alloway, and L. Krames [AGK94]. The authors report on the use of a simulation tool called Sniffy to teach Skinner's experiment concerning operant conditioning to 900 undergraduate psychology students. The stand-alone program uses 2.5D visualization. Its purpose is to visualize and communicate the methods of training, shaping, acquisition, and extinction of conditioned behavior. Referring to their particular scenario, the authors also stress the financial advantages of using computer-based simulations for this classical laboratory experiment, as compared to the budget required for the acquisition and maintenance of laboratories and animal facilities.

With regard to Article 1 of the United Nations Educational, Scientific, and Cultural Organization's (UNESCO) charter on the Preservation of the Digital Heritage [UNE03] and the statutes of the International Council of Museums (ICOM) [ICO01], reconstructed historical psychological key experiments are considered both digital heritage and exhibition objects in a virtual museum for the purpose of study and education.

This thesis contributes to the following central topics:

- Development of a theoretical approach for the synthesis of replicated (historical and non-historical) virtual laboratories that allow the conduction of *interactive* and *reversible* psychological experiments based on deterministic or non-deterministic *simulation models*.

- Implementation of psychological experiments in virtual 3D environments, based on this approach.

- Development of a metaphorical design for and implementation of a 3D virtual museum framework system for these replicated experiments.

The following five psychological topics (listed with the researcher's name) have been selected in cooperation with members of the department of psychology:

1. Operant conditioning (B.F. Skinner),

2. Forgetting curve (H. Ebbinghaus),

3. Cognitive maps (E.C. Tolman),

4. Functional fixedness (K. Duncker), and

5. Iconic memory (G. Sperling).

The corresponding historical experiments have been replicated in 3D environments through application of the theoretical approach (modeling pipeline). Apart from their historical impact on the development of psychology as a science, each implementation focuses on different aspects of the proposed theoretical approach. Skinner's experiment has been implemented using a non-deterministic behavior model based on Markov chains that controls the "behavior" of a virtual lab rat. A deterministic finite state model has been used in the replication of Duncker's experiment. The replication of Ebbinghaus' historical experiment describes the successful integration of a special hardware input device (concept keyboard). While the replication of Tolman's experiment demonstrates the integration of a database for position tracking, Sperling's experiment focuses on the integration of existing 2D content in a 3D environment.

In addition to the model synthesis approach, metaphorical design considerations are discussed resulting in a theoretical approach for the design of parameterizable conceptional and temporal metaphors that allow the structured spatial and temporal arrangement of 2D and 3D content. The implementation uses dynamically generated conceptual metaphors and template-based temporal metaphors. Finally, a structural model for a virtual environment for replicated experiments is proposed, which is not limited to psychology-related content.

The resulting system is referred to as the **Replicave** system (**Replica**tion of classical psychological experiments in **v**irtual **e**nvironments), which is a web-based virtual 3D museum environment that consists of a modular framework system and various replicated laboratories based on the aforementioned five psychological historical key experiments. The above-mentioned research project also lead to an alternative 2D only implementation by the department of psychology [Wor04].

The question whether users prefer 2D or 3D as well as the 3D user interface have been focused in an evaluation, which has revealed that users prefer 3D-based visualization in the case of the Skinner experiment[2].

---

[2]The Skinner experiment represents the only experiment that has been implemented in both 2D and 3D versions and allowed a comparison.

The Replicave system demonstrates the feasibility of applying a newly developed modeling pipeline and a structural model for a virtual environment for replicated experiments that results in the implementation of a dynamic and interactive web-based virtual 3D museum environment, which represents a constructivist learning environment in the domain of psychology as well as a virtual museum that contributes to the preservation of digital heritage.

1.2 Outline of the thesis

An overview about current web-based 3D modeling and rendering technologies is given in Chapter 2 focusing on the Virtual Reality Modeling Language (VRML).

In Chapter 3, the definition of a *virtual museum* is extended by replicated virtual environments that incorporate the key concepts of interactivity, reversibility, and simulation. Thereafter, the theoretical modeling pipeline is introduced together with a model synthesis for replicated virtual laboratories. In addition, metaphorical design considerations are discussed for the arrangement of these replicated (historical and non-historical) virtual environments within a virtual museum framework, which is proposed as a structure model of a virtual environment for replicated laboratories.

Chapter 4 covers the implementation of the framework system. Chapter 5 outlines the implementation of the historical experiments, based on the model synthesis described in Chapter 3. Chapter 6 provides an evaluation of the framework system. Finally, Chapter 7 provides a discussion of the results achieved.

Chapter 2

Web-based 3D modeling and rendering technologies

2.1 Introduction

In this chapter, an overview is given on basic modeling techniques, modeling languages, programming/scripting languages, and graphics APIs that are presently available for the design and implementation of a web-based 3D system. A schematic overview is given in Figure 2.1.

The 3D modeling languages are grouped by their modeling technique. Geometry and image based modeling languages and rendering techniques are presented with references to existing implementations. In addition, hybrid approaches of these two methods are presented. Then, the 3D rendering application programming interfaces (APIs) DirectX and OpenGL are summarized. Thereafter, related programming and markup languages are mentioned that offer required enhanced features, such as additional interaction (Flash), special computational capabilities (Java), or web browser enhancement (plug-in detection). Finally, geometry and image based modeling and rendering are summarized in a table that serves as a decision matrix.

For reasons of completeness, hardware-related components are mentioned in Figure 2.1. However, I/O interfaces and graphics hardware are not covered in detail. If the deployment of hardware interfaces, other than standard keyboard or mice, should be required, the manufacturer's APIs or software development kits (SDK) should be consulted. As these are often under development, proprietary, or only distributed commercially, they are not covered in this section.

7

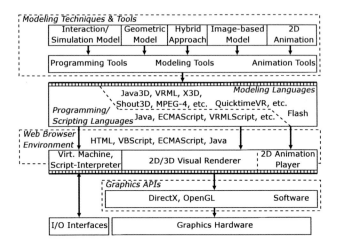

Figure 2.1: Modeling techniques, programming/scripting languages, and graphics APIs (overview)

2.2   Geometry based modeling and rendering

2.2.1   Java3D

Java3D is an object oriented 3D API by Sun Microsystems Inc., based on Java. Hardware accelerated 3D graphics rendering is realized by falling back on the low level APIs OpenGL and DirectX although the latter two can not be accessed directly within Java3D. 3D scenes are described and referred to in a *scene graph* model. Support for external interfaces (input devices and surround sound) is included. In his book "Java 3D programming" , D. Selman gives an overview on Java3D but also indicates performance issues with both the 3D rendering engine and the Java garbage collector [Sel02]. Finally, the author recommends to implement high performance 3D applications in other languages (that is, OpenGL or C).

B. Nill implemented an interactive reconstruction of the Schickard calculator from 1623 in Java3D, based on geometric 3D modeling [Nil99]. Since the only existing prototype of the historical calculator was destroyed in 1624, Nill's virtual reconstruction is based on primary sources (that is, letters written by Schickard in which the inventor describes the construction design), on drafts and descriptions from secondary sources, and on a physical reconstruction from 1960 that is kept in a museum in Tübingen/Germany. Nonetheless, tests with other existing Java3D applications under Microsoft Windows 2000 have shown stability and perform-

ance issues in large and complex virtual worlds[1]. Furthermore, Java3D requires
the installation of three different software packages before an application can be
started on this platform: Sun's Java runtime environment (JRE), Sun's Java3D
for Windows runtime for JRE, and the Java3D application itself, all of which are
not included in a default MS Windows installation.

2.2.2 VRML

The "Virtual Reality Modelling Language" (VRML) is a plain text hierarchical
scene graph description language that defines the behaviour and geometry of a
3D scene ("world") and the way a user can navigate through it. VRML world
files have the file extension .wrl (or .wrz for gzip compressed files) and require
either a stand-alone application or a web browser plug-in to be displayed.

A VRML file describes a 3D world through a directed acyclic graph (*scene graph*)
and its nodes. In VRML 2.0 and later, node types include geometry primitives,
appearance properties, sensors, and scripts. Nodes contain individual properties
that are called *fields*. A basic event architecture (*routing*) supports node-to-
node communication within the scene graph. Various *Interpolator* nodes can be
linked with *TimeSensor* nodes and allow animations. Modularisation and code
re-usability is supported by a prototyping concept which can not considered an
object-oriented concept. An object-oriented extension of VRML 2.0 is presented
in Section 2.2.6. A complete reference of nodes, fields and events is given in the
book "The Annotated VRML 2.0 Reference Manual" by R. Carey and G. Bell
[BC97a]. In the past, the naming and version policy of VRML was not consistent.
A short overview of the history of VRML and its various standards is given in
the following paragraph.

2.2.2.1 History of the VRML specification

VRML emerged from the OpenInventor file format developed for a research project at Silicon Graphics, Inc. in 1989 [BC97a]. The first draft of the VRML 1.0
specification was published in late 1994 and featured primitive 3D objects, multiple light sources and hyperlinks [AF98]. In August 1996, the VRML 2.0 specification was released which added sound, interaction, animation, scripting and
prototyping support. Scripting is supported through the *Script* node that, once
triggered by an event, allows the execution of a code in ECMAScript (a synonym for JavaScript) or Java bytecode. The initial idea of VRMLScript support,
defined as a subset of JavaScript, was abandoned in favor of full ECMAScript
support.

In 1997, a revised version of VRML 2.0 was submitted for approval to the International Organisation for Standardisation (ISO). The revised VRML 2.0 spe-

---

[1]This includes Sun's "fly through" demo. http://java.sun.com/products/java-media/
3D/flythrough.html [Accessed 22 February 2006]

cification was called VRML97 and was standardised by the International Electro-
technical Commission (IEC) and the ISO (ISO/IEC 14772-1:1997). In annex B
of this standard, the scripting reference for Java bytecode introduces methods for
external access to the *Script* node.

Although a first proposal for a standardised interface for external access was
issued in 1996, it was not until 2002 that the the external authoring interface
(EAI) was formally added as an extension to the already existing standard as
ISO/IEC 14772-2:2002. Many VRML browsers already supported the EAI before
2002 and VRML97 did not change its name after the extension of the standard.
Hence, VRML97 is a synonym for the complete 2002 ISO/IEC 14772 standard.

In 2000, the Web3D consortium began to work on a revised version of VRML97.
Several revisions of the new specification were published as ISO/ IEC 14772:200x,
also referred to as "VRML200x", although the specification included the propos-
ition to ask the ISO for a formal renaming to "X3D" (see Section 2.2.3).

2.2.2.2   External authoring interface (EAI)

The external authoring interface (EAI) is a standard that defines an API for
external applications, including Java applets, to communicate with a VRML
browser. There are four run-time access types supported by the EAI[2]:

- Full access to the *browser script interface*[3].

- Sending events to *EventIn* nodes within a scene graph (for example, triggering events).

- Reading the last value sent from the *EventOut* nodes of a scene graph.

- *Notification* of changes in values of node *fields* due to events.

Unlike the *Script* node, the modifying application itself is not a part of the scene
graph. While a *field* value can be directly read or written by an external application, it is noteworthy, that the processing of a VRML *event* cascade is handled
exclusively by the VRML browser. To the external application, the event processing mechanism appears as a black box: although it can send (that is, initiate)
events and read their outcome (that is, read the last value sent from an *EventOut*
node), it can not control the internal event processing.

The EAI defines an open standard that allows the integration of high level programming languages for scene graph control and a more efficient implementation
of complex data structures and algorithms, as compared to ECMAScript. It is
usually implemented in Java (see Section 2.6.2) and referred to as the Java-EAI.

---

[2]http://www.web3d.org/x3d/specifications/vrml/ISO-IEC-14772-VRML97/part2/
concepts.html [Accessed 22 February 2006]
[3]http://www.web3d.org/x3d/specifications/vrml/ISO-IEC-14772-VRML97/part1/
concepts.html [Accessed 22 February 2006]

2.2.2.3 Implementation examples

Implementations of web-based virtual museums include the Living Virtual Museum Online [ASRN01] that was produced jointly by the Fraunhofer Institute for Software and Systems Engineering (ISST), the German Historical Museum in Berlin, and the *Haus der Geschichte* of the Federal Republic of Germany in Bonn. The project seeks to create a multimedia information system on twentieth-century German history. Various options for accessing its information are presented, including 3D spaces with reproduced 3D objects and further multimedia documents on historical events[4]. Although the content is presented in a historical context, most exhibition objects are static and non-interactive.

Examples of virtual 3D experimental environments include applications in the military and health domain. A web-based 3D experimental tool that allows an interactive control of an animated pre-defined military scenario is described in the paper "Web-Based 3D Reconstruction of Scenarios for Limited Objective Experiments" by C. Blais *et al.* [BBHW02]. One scenario was reconstructed from publicly available descriptions of an authentic scenario, the terrorist attack on USS Cole. Thereafter, the authors describe a visual 2D editor for the creation of similar threat scenarios and a 3D implementation, based on VRML and Java, that allows analyst-versus-analyst interactions to scrutinize scenario possibilities and analyze alternative realities.

2.2.3 X3D

X3D (Extensible 3D) is an XML-based extension of VRML97 proposed by the Web3D Consortium. At present, there are three X3D-related international standards[5] with corresponding FDIS (Final Proposed Draft Amendment) or CD (Committee Draft), respectively[6]:

1. ISO/IEC 19775:2004 contains the definition of the abstract functional specification for the X3D framework and its standardized components and profiles, and the definition of the scene access interface (SAI) which can be used to interact with X3D worlds both from within the worlds or from external programs.

2. ISO/IEC 19776:2005 defines the data encoding specification (XML, VRML, binary) of X3D for XML.

3. ISO/IEC FDIS 19777:2005 specifies the bindings of the X3D language to ECMAScript and the Java programming language for use in X3D internal representation (*Script* nodes) and for external application access.

---

[4]http://www.dhm.de/lemo/ [Accessed 22 February 2006]
[5]http://www.web3d.org/x3d/specifications/x3d_specification.html [Accessed 22 February 2006]
[6]http://www.web3d.org/x3d/specifications/ [Accessed 22 February 2006]

Summarizing, the main features of X3D are:

- Backward compatibility to VRML97

- XML-based language

- Modularization (through different profiles)

- Extensibility

As an XML-based language, X3D demands stricter code conformance than its predecessor. It is defined as a lightweight core that describes the basic 3D rendering components (geometry model, lighting model, and event handling). The core can be extended by adding components. A component is a set of nodes or an extended code implementation that defines special functionalities. A profile is a subset of components and must be defined in an X3D file to specify the capabilities needed by a 3D world. There are various predefined profiles: *Core*, *Interchange*, *Interactive*, *Immersive*, and *Full*. The *Immersive* profile is supposed to deliver VRML97 backward compatibility.

X3D authoring tools include any XML editor or X3D-Edit[7] by the X3D Working Group. X3D-Edit is based on the Xeena XML editor by IBM[8] and is implemented in Sun Java3D and Sun Java (see Sections 2.2.1 and 2.6.2). X3D-Edit features a VRML97 file import filter that is based on the Vrml97ToX3d-Translator by Wang [Wan02].

At present, available "X3D browsers" display X3D worlds based on the *immersive* profile, the code is converted to VRML97 code by using XSL stylesheets and displayed by a native VRML97 browser.

The Java-based toolkit Xj3D by the Web3D Consortium is an ongoing project that was initially intended to create a file loader for the Java3D API. After more than five years of development, it aims to provide a fully compliant implementation of the VRML97 and X3D specifications. Although the Xj3D "milestone" releases include a 3D browser, the software is still in an experimental state. It requires manual system configuration (for example, setting of environment variables) and is still not fully VRML97 compliant. Especially, multimedia and interaction related node types, such as *PlaneSensor*, *Sound*, *MovieTexture*, *Text*, and *TouchSensor* are not fully implemented yet. Besides, the problems of the Java3D rendering engine, mentioned in 2.2.1, are to be considered.

The advantages of X3D are its backward compatibility to VRML97 and its flexible profile-based architecture that - theoretically - allows a sustainable and individual system design without dependence on proprietary extensions to the standard. Although Bitmanagement Software GmbH and Parallelgraphics Inc. provide basic

---

[7]http://www.web3d.org/x3d/content/README.X3D-Edit.html [Accessed 22 February 2006]

[8]http://alphaworks.ibm.com/tech/xeena[Accessed 22 February 2006]

X3D support in their 3D browser products, VRML97 files that use complex event routing and proprietary node types are not covered by the present X3D profiles. A drawback of X3D is the lack of native 3D modelers and browsers, that support the new X3D-specific node types. In most cases, X3D code is simply generated by translating VRML97 data.

2.2.4 Shout3D

Shout3D is a combination of a 3D description language that uses the corresponding Java-based Shout3D player. Shout3D (file extension: .s3d) is a subset of VRML97 (see Section 2.2.2) that is extended by proprietary nodes[9]. The commercial viewer applet software is sold per domain and year, focusing on plug-in free 3D product presentation for e-Commerce.

3D modeling tools that provide a Shout3D file export filter include 3D Studio Max and Spazz3D by Virtock Technologies. Alternatively, any text editor can be used to modify a VRML97 file to match the Shout3D format.

2.2.5 Macromedia Shockwave3D

In 2001, Macromedia[10] published version 8.5 of its development suite Director Shockwave Studio with 3D authoring capability, called Shockwave3D. It focused on web-based 3D content, virtual warehouses, and the B2C market. While the proprietary plug-in is free, Director Studio is a commercial product.

Even on 3D hardware accelerated graphics cards, several 3D display tests with the Shockwave Player showed that the response time during interaction was very high (up to 3 seconds). Besides, the plug-in was unstable, even when displaying a small amount of objects.

2.2.6 VRML++

In 1997, St. Diehl published an object-oriented extension to VRML 2.0 called VRML++ that aimed to increase re-usability, readability, and extensibility by adding features of object-orientation: a class and inheritance model, inclusion polymorphism, an improved type system, abstract classes, and dynamic routing and binding [Die97]. There is no native browser for VRML++ files. Instead, a preprocessor converts VRML++ code into VRML 2.0, JavaScript, and VRMLScript including support for the mentioned features. Although VRML++

---

[9]http://web.archive.org/web/20030606200252/www.eyematic.com/products_shout3d.html [Accessed 22 January 2004]

[10]http://www.macromedia.com/ [Accessed 22 February 2006]

is a promising approach to create VRML based content more efficiently and despite the fact that Diehl published code examples [Die98], the language was not widely accepted.

2.2.7   MPEG-4/BIFS

BIFS (**BI**nary **F**ormat for **S**cenes) provides a framework for the MPEG-4 (ISO/IEC 14496) presentation engine that consists of a set of operational scene elements (*nodes*), a binary data structure, the *BIFS Command*, and the *BIFS Anim* protocol.

With BIFS, both 2D and 3D MPEG-4 compliant data objects (that is, media content) can be organized, stored and transmitted in a single data format. The composition nodes of BIFS and the scene graph concept were based on the VRML 2.0 specification. Hence, BIFS supports the complete VRML 2.0 node set and routing mechanism. Furthermore, BIFS also features support for additional node types (2D objects, 3D audio), dynamic scene description (real-time object creation, modification, and destruction), data compression, streaming, and an integrated timing model for media synchronization.

MPEG-4 scenes are distributed by streaming the scene description and media objects separately, which allows dynamic object operations (for example, node insertion) by updating the scene description. The required operational commands are defined in the *BIFS Command* protocol. The *BIFS Anim* protocol features extensions for animation control.

Authoring an MPEG-4 scene is accomplished in three steps. First, any 2D or 3D media content has to be created and stored in data formats that are supported by the MPEG-4 bitstream compiler. Ideally, all content files are in the MPEG-4 format. In a second step, the scene is described in a plain text file. Three ASCII text formats can be used for scene authoring: BIFS-Text, XMT-A, and XMT-Ω [KWC00]. Finally, the scene description text file and all media content files are compiled to MPEG-4 by an appropriate converter.

A more detailed overview on the MPEG-4 standard, including converters and players, is given in [PE02].

2.3   Image based modeling and rendering

A disadvantage of the traditional modeling/rendering pipeline using geometric primitives is that both 3D modeling and real-time[11] rendering of photo-realistic scenes are expensive.

---

[11]The term "real-time" is meant to express a low latency (that is, less than 1/25 sec.) between the rendered frames.

In image based rendering (IBR), different views are rendered from an environmental representation based on high-resolution images (for example, photographs) instead of a geometric polygon based model. Image based modeling refers to the process of defining a scene by adequately locating a discrete set of 2D images.

The advantages are a modest computational complexity of display algorithms and a constant rendering time that is independent of the scene's complexity. Due to the photorealistic nature of the input images, the rendering engine produces high quality images. However, rendering images for arbitrary viewpoints requires a large amount of input images and the maximal resolution is limited by the quality of the original images. Even after using data compression, photo-realistic IBR still requires a relatively large amount of data.

Many IBR algorithms rely on partial 3D scene reconstruction and require depth coordinates which can be generated by any of the following techniques:

- *User input:* Depth information can be manually assigned by the user although this requires the user's comprehension of the scene layout. In a paper entitled "Image-based modeling and photo editing", B.M. Oh, M. Chen, J. Dorsey, and F. Durand discuss an image-based modeling system that includes a user controlled depth assignment tool suited especially for monocular images [OCDD01].

- *Depth estimation:* When using binocular (that is, stereoscopic) or trinocular input images, depth can be estimated by various methods and a depth or disparity map can be calculated. In a paper entitled "Dense Disparity Map Estimation Respecting Image Discontinuities: A PDE and Scale-Space Based Approach" [ADSW00], Alvarez *et al.* give a review of existing approaches and discuss an energy based strategy.

- *Depth scanning:* Laser range scanners deliver native 4D input images including depth coordinates.

Once a sufficient amount of depth coordinates is available, a pixel based 3D model of the scene can be defined. The following three sections summarize standard IBR techniques:

2.3.1 Environment mapping

An environment map $I(k,l) = L_{P_{obj}}(\overrightarrow{x})\ k,l \in \mathbb{R}, \overrightarrow{x} \in \mathbb{R}^3$ stores the incoming light from all direction at a given point P_{obj}. Originally, environment mapping is used as a texturing method in geometry based rendering to visualize the reflection of an object's environment on its surface. In IBR, P_{obj} is interpreted as a fixed view point giving an outward look $I(k,l)$ on the environment at arbitrary orientations. In practice, a cylindrical, planar, cubic, or spherical environment map is calculated from either a prerendered scene, a professional panoramic camera, or by stitching a finite sequence of overlapping photographs taken from a fixed viewpoint. Then, rendering is the process of reprojecting the environment map.

Stitching refers to the patchwork metaphor and describes the process of combining the overlapping 2D images according to their correspondence. Basically, this is a problem of finding adequate control points for any pair of corresponding images and approximating a continuous transition of colour, brightness, and contrast. Commercial stitching tools include "RealViz Stitcher"[12] and "VRToolbox VR Worx"[13]. The mentioned products feature advanced computer graphics algorithms including automatic colour, brightness, and contrast equalisation and lens distortion management. "Autopano-sift" [Now04] is an open sourced[14] tool to stitch and edit immersive 360° panoramic images. It implements pattern recognition algorithms and automatic control point definition for any finite number of arbitrary photographs based on the *scale invariant feature transform* (SIFT) detection method by D. Lowe [Low99]. Lowe's method is invariant to image scaling, translation, rotation, and partially invariant to affine or 3D projection.

Rendering images is done by reprojecting the visible areas and displaying them on the view plane. When using spherical environment maps, non-linear image warping has to be applied. Some web-based solutions based on environment mapping are presented in the following sections.

The four disadvantages of the environment mapping technique are the limited number of viewpoints, the huge amount of data required for photorealism, the non-dynamic character of the scene, and the high cost of applying changes to the scene. In order to obtain a high degree of spatial realism, many viewpoints have to be generated and hyperlinked using photo-realistic images that require a large amount of data. While this usually does not affect 3D worlds that are stored on local or removable media (for example, CD-/DVD-ROM), web based systems have to be optimized in terms of image resolution and amount of viewpoints. The rendered scenes display a static world without animated objects. Interactivity is limited to changing the orientation or, optionally, selecting another static predefined viewpoint. Finally, changes made in the model have to be applied to all affected images which may yield to a high workload since images have to be either retaken or digitally reworked.

Recording an panoramic movie requires a panorama capable tripod with sufficient degrees of freedom. Some digital cameras in the consumer market feature panoramic picture support although using a stationary tripod should be preferred.

---

[12]http://www.realviz.com/products/st/ [Accessed 22 February 2006]

[13]http://www.vrtoolbox.com/vrthome.html [Accessed 22 February 2006]

[14]Although autopano-sift is open sourced, its licence states that any commercial application of the software might require a licence of the University of British Columbia, Canada.

2.3.1.1 QTVR (camera rotation)

Apple's QuicktimeVR (QTVR) [Che95] generates panoramic views by reprojecting stitched images on a cylinder or cubic surface. The fixed camera position is located in the center of the corresponding projection object providing an outward view by camera rotation. Cylindrical, "fish eye", or wide angled planar reprojection is used for vertically limited panoramic images allowing a maximum viewing angle of 180° in vertical and 360° in the horizontal direction. For omni-directional 360° panoramic images, cubic or spherical environment maps are used.

Image display and camera control is implemented in the QTVR player which can also be embedded into HTML documents. Virtual worlds are built by aligning adjacent viewpoints in a grid and connecting them with so called *"hot spots"* (anchors) that refer to another corresponding (that is, neighboring) QTVR image when clicked by the user. As a result, QTVR is capable of building large scale virtual worlds, although the impression of a continuous camera movement can only be accomplished with a fine grid which results in an inadequate amount of image data.

In order to optimize the download transmission time, web based QTVR offers content streaming in different qualities: first, a low resolution image is loaded and displayed on the web client. Hereafter, a high resolution image is downloaded and overlaid. Image regions can be focused by a zoom function. QTVR implements a smoothing filter that helps to reduce pixel artifacts if the image resolution is insufficient.

The advantage of QTVR is its ability to render high quality 3D environments in relatively short time. Although the number of predefined viewpoints (and hence the user navigation) is limited, a QTVR based world with adequately chosen viewpoints provides a good technique for presenting photo realistic static 3D environments. Among the existing QTVR based implementations are museums[15], buildings[16], and landscapes[17].

2.3.1.2 iSee Photovista Panorama

The authoring tool Photovista Panorama by iSeeMedia[18] (formerly: LivePicture) is a complete commercial solution for web-based panoramic imaging: The tool can export panoramic images to either Quicktime compatible files or to Java applets that can instantly be embedded in any web page to display immersive content without the need to install any native 3D plug-in. Compared to their Quicktime counterpart, the Java applets do not feature *streaming* and *hyperlinking*.

---

[15]http://www.louvre.or.jp/louvre/QTVR/anglais/index.htm [Accessed 22 February 2006]

[16]Markus Nachtrab's virtual presentation of the Einsteinturm in Potsdam/Germany: http://www.zursonneempor.de/ [Accessed 22 February 2006]

[17]http://www.kaidan.com/media/summerland.mov [Accessed 22 February 2006]

[18]http://www.iseephotovista.com/ [Accessed 22 February 2006]

2.3.1.3   PanoramaTools

PanoramaTools [Der01] is an open sourced panorama picture software collection for creation, editing and distributing immersive 360° panoramic images. It includes tools for stitching, creating stereographic images, morphing, and automatic colour and brightness adjustment. The PTViewer is a free and platform-independent Java applet for spherical panoramic viewing which can use free extensions to display QTVR movies. A user-friendly GUI for the command-based PanoramaTools is called "hugin"[19].

2.3.2   View interpolation

View interpolation covers the field of interpolation based algorithms that predict and render new interjacent images for new viewpoints from a discrete sequence of existing images.

In a paper entitled "3-D Scene Representation as a Collection of Images and Fundamental Matrices", Faugeras and Laveau discuss a model and an image prediction algorithm that renders new images without the necessity to reengineer a complete 3D scene [FL94]. The authors use algebraic relations and computer vision algorithms to bypass a computationally expensive 3D reconstruction.

In the context of web based 3D systems, the following aspects of view interpolation should be considered: it is computationally expensive, it offers an approach to approximate the image of an object from arbitrary orbiting viewpoints, but the interpolation may cause quality issues. Since the output image I_1 is an interpolated image supposed to approximate the real view I_2, the difference $d(I_1, I_2)$ between both images may exceed a tolerable limit. The approximation may then result in uncontrollable loss (for example, previously hidden surfaces should be visible but are not displayed) or gain (for example, surfaces are displayed at a wrong position) of important information and affect the user's perception of a given scene.

Object rotation

An object with a transparent or fixed-colored background can be presented by displaying a movie that has been recorded by orbiting a camera around the convex hull of a fixed still object focusing the same. This process is also called object rotation because it is equivalent to rotating the object in front of a stationary camera. Since recording an object rotation results in an array of images taken from mutually different camera positions, environment maps can not be applied.

---

[19]http://hugin.sourceforge.net/ [Accessed 23 January 2004]

2.3.2.1   QTVR (object rotation)

QTVR also features object rotation. As Chen [Che95] points out, the camera positions are aligned along an orbital grid with longitude and latitude coordinates. For a continuous movie display, the distance between two neighbouring camera positions should be constant in the grid. The result is a bidirectional graph with image nodes along which the user can navigate, that is, the user is examining the object. Optionally, QTVR can store different images for different viewing directions. In this case, the graph becomes directional.

In fact, QTVR does not calculate new images for interleaving camera positions but simply approximates them by quantizing them to the nearest grid point. Hence, this feature requires a narrow grid for an adequate object representation. Chen mentions an increment of 10 degrees.

As mentioned above, there are two methods to create a so called object movie. First, a camera is orbited around a stationary object. In this case, a camera is mounted on an object rig with sufficient degrees of freedom from which it takes photographs of the object. Second, the object is rotated on a turntable in front of a stationary camera.

Object rotation is applicable for presenting small static objects only. Since all views are stored in an image array, the amount of data required for a high quality 360°×360° object movie has to be considered as relatively high. Recording an object movie requires professional photographic studio equipment including lighting and backgrounds causing additional production costs.

An implementation that uses QTVR object rotation is the EUR 750.000 virtual museum project "Karlsruher Türkenbeute"[20].

2.3.3   Light field rendering

The light field is defined as the radiance at a given point in a given direction for an occlusion-free space. Hence, the technique can be applied to display objects with a convex hull or to generate views of occlusion free rooms or spaces (for example, fly through of an architectural models or outdoor scenes). In their paper "Light field rendering"[LH96], M. Levoy and P. Hanrahan propose an interpolation technique based on a 4D plenoptic function. The authors describe the creation of a light field from both static images and model based environments and methods to limit the amount of data required to efficiently reconstruct views from arbitrary positions. The Stanford university Computer Graphics Laboratory has published a viewer (lifview), an authoring tool (lifauth), and example light fields[21]. In their paper "Hardware-accelerated Dynamic Light Field Rendering", B. Goldlücke,

---

[20]http://www.tuerkenbeute.de/ [Accessed 22 February 2006]
[21]http://graphics.stanford.edu/software/lightpack/lightpack.html [Accessed 22 February 2006]

M. Magnor, and B. Wilburn describe a method to record and render light fields for dynamic scenes [GMW02].

Light field rendering offers an approach for creating photorealistic 3D objects and exploratory 3D environments. In practice, the authoring process is complex and expensive, the large amount of data makes it unsuitable for web based applications, and event handling (for advanced interactivity) is not supported by any of the available viewers.

2.4   Hybrid approaches

Considering geometry and image based rendering, hybrid approaches were developed to blend the advantages of both models.

2.4.1   3D prototyping

In 3D prototyping, 3D scenes are rendered by a combination of a simplified or approximated geometric model and high quality textures that are extracted, transformed, and projected from a sequence of images onto the corresponding object surfaces. Like in image based modeling, a scene's detail quality depends on the quality of the input images, whereas the depth information given by the plain geometric model allows fast scene rendering from arbitrary viewpoints.

In practice, triangular or planar quadrangular surfaces in a simple geometric model are mapped onto corresponding convex polygons in a photograph by mapping control points. For each surface, shearing, scaling, rotation, and transformation algorithms extract the adequate textures from the images, allowing a fast and high quality texturing. Depth information is defined by user input. In contrary to the stitching process described in Section 2.3.1, the calculation of disparity or depth maps is not needed.

Due to the simplicity of the geometric model and the cost of manual control point definition, 3D prototyped scenes are commonly used in applications that require a low or medium level of detail or in which a high level of detail is restricted to regions of interest, such as:

- *Arts and architecture:* Art historian K. Kaldenbach used 3D prototyping to generate both a 3D model of the historical city of Delft and fly-through movies focusing on historical buildings which are depicted on selected drawings by Dutch painter Johannes Vermeer (1632-1675). Kaldenbach points out that, for the first project, historical city maps were used to define object polygons in the xz-plane, the height of each building (y-value) was defined manually, and other details (including textures) were applied according to old photographs, paintings by other artists, or other sources [Kal99]. In the second project, several fly-through movies were rendered from a geometric model and its corresponding textures that were extracted from Vermeer's drawings and additional images of the selected historically important buildings [Kal00b]. Kaldenbach considers the application of virtual reality in both projects to be appealing for experienced art historians as well as for persons who "hardly ever visit fine art museums"[Kal00a].

- *Augmented reality:* 3D prototyping is used to generate photorealistic 3D backgrounds for various augmented reality applications (entertainment, education, scientific visualization).

A very popular 3D prototyping product, also used in Kaldenbach's project "Walking with Vermeer", was Canoma by MetaCreations. The company was acquired by Adobe. Parts of the Canoma software have been included in Adobe Atmosphere and, meanwhile, in Acrobat 3D[22].

2.4.2 3D surface model reconstruction

3D surface model reconstruction summarizes methods that use image data to reconstruct a detailed geometric scene model of all visible surfaces and their photorealistic textures. The procedure usually involves: acquisition of an image sequence, calibration, projective reconstruction, depth map calculation, and 3D model generation. Once a model has been generated, textures can be applied, like in 3D prototyping.

3D surface reconstruction combines the accuracy of a complex geometric 3D model with the photorealism of image-based techniques. Unless the scene model is postedited manually or with advanced 3D pattern matching algorithms, only the visible object surfaces are reconstructed.

As described in Section 2.3, the depth map can be either estimated or - if a laser range scanner is used - measured. However, both methods tend to deliver a high number of vertices resulting and a significant amount of 3D data.

There are abundant examples of reconstructed sites in archeology. In his doctoral thesis entitled "Self-calibration and metric 3D reconstruction from uncalibrated image sequences", M. Pollefeys demonstrates the 3D reconstruction of the archaeological site of Sagalossos/Turkey in various VRML models by using uncalibrated image sequences[23]. Furthermore, archaeological building hypotheses can be visualized by combining the model derived from the image-based technique with other predefined geometric models [Pol99, p. 159]. In this case, 3D surface model reconstruction fulfills two main tasks:

- Texture recording: In accordance with other methods based on image data, 3D surface modeling algorithms can generate photorealistic surface textures if the given image resolution is sufficient.

---

[22]http://www.adobe.com/products/acrobat3d/main.html [Accessed 22 February 2006]
[23]http://www.esat.kuleuven.ac.be/psi/sagalossos/ [Accessed 23 February 2006]

- 3D model data acquisition: Given a sufficient resolution, a normalized geometric 3D model generated by 3D surface reconstruction can be used to measure or sufficiently approximate any euclidean distance, instead of using time-consuming manual measuring instruments. Since 3D surface reconstruction is scale-independent, this application includes digital terrain mapping as well as surface modeling of small objects. However, the accuracy of the 3D model depends on the resolution and quality of the input images.

The method's advantage, as compared to plain geometric based approaches, is its time-efficiency. On the other hand, the generated amount of 3D model and image textures data is often too high for low bandwidth web-based applications and 3D objects are neither modeled nor stored in the form of geometric primitives. Due to its limitation on static surfaces, the modeling of occluded surfaces (for example, surfaces that become exposed by triggering an animation) requires manual post-editing of the geometric model.

Finally, 3D surface model reconstruction can be combined with pattern recognition algorithms that analyze 3D data sets with the intention to recognize surface shapes that can be expressed by geometric primitives or by complex objects that are stored in an advanced geometric object library.

2.4.3   Large-scale 3D model acquisition

Another method to achieve photorealistic rendering of real world objects is texturing a simple geometric model with viewpoint-dependent images. In their paper entitled "Data Processing Algorithms for Generating Textured 3D Building Facade Meshes from Laser Scans and Camera Images", C. Früh, S. Jain, and A. Zakhor describe a method for capturing a real world 3D city model and corresponding textures with two inexpensive airborne 2D laser scanners and cameras [FJZ05]. By processing gathered data with appropriate algorithms, a simple geometric 3D model (mesh) is generated. By synchronizing the camera with the laser scanners and calibrating both systems, the each 3D vertex can be mapped to its corresponding pixel, allowing an accurate reconstruction of both geometric model and surface textures. The approach was successfully tested with a city landscape scene and offers a cost-effective method for the ground-based rendering of large-scale real world scenes, as they are used for virtual landmark-related psychological experiments.

As already mentioned, the amount of data required for such large-scale scenes (image data and 3D model data, respectively) should be considered with regard to web-based applications.

2.5   Rendering interfaces

In this section, the two rendering APIs OpenGL and DirectX are introduced, as they are located in the layer between a 3D application and the 3D graphics hardware. On present PCs, hardware-accelerated 3D graphics rendering is usually accomplished by either one of the two APIs.

2.5.1   OpenGL

OpenGL ("Open Graphics Library") is a hardware-independent core API to 2D and 3D graphics hardware that includes about 200 distinct commands to specify objects and operations needed to produce interactive graphics (mainly 3D) applications. Based on the IRIS GL by Silicon Graphics Inc. (SGI), Microsoft and SGI decided to support OpenGL as a graphics standard in 1992. OpenGL is based on a client/server architecture with a standardized protocol: drawing commands are requested by the client and received by the server that performs the commands.

A 3D model has to be build up from a small set of geometric primitives - points, lines, and polygons. Other relevant features are: accumulation buffering, depth buffering, alpha blending, scene camera, color indices, level of detail (LOD) control for mipmap textures, 3D textures, lighting, shading, pixel operations, and transformations.

OpenGL can be extended to support event handling and high level commands by libraries that implement advanced features and allow more complicated shapes. Among the commonly used OpenGL related libraries are:

- The *OpenGL Utility Library* (GLU): GLU[24] contains several routines that use lower-level OpenGL commands to perform tasks as setting up matrices for specific viewing orientations and projections, performing polygon tessellation, and rendering complex surfaces such as cylinders, spheres, free-form surfaces, and NURBS (Non-Uniform Rational B-Spline) surfaces. The library is distributed as part of many OpenGL implementations.

- The *OpenGL Utility Toolkit* (GLUT): GLUT[25] is a window system independent[26] extension for handling OpenGL windows on an underlying window system. It includes support for multiple rendering windows, overlay management, callback driven event processing, event handling of input devices such as mouse or keyboard, timers, a basic pop up menu facility,

---

[24]http://www.opengl.org/documentation/specs/glu/glu1_3.pdf [Accessed 22 February 2006]

[25]http://www.opengl.org/documentation/specs/glut/spec3/spec3.html [Accessed 22 February 2006]

[26]GLUT currently exists for MS Windows, Mac OS, and the X Window System.

and bitmap and vector font support. For professional applications, other platform dependent advanced libraries such as *OpenGL for Microsoft Windows* (WGL) for Microsoft Windows based systems or GLX for Unix-based systems may be used.

Due to its portable and modular structure, OpenGL has become a standard on all major platforms and is commonly used by many 3D applications including games, scientific visualization, and VRML browser plug-ins. OpenGL specifications are governed by the Architecture Review Board (ARB), an industry consortium of leading graphics vendors. The ARB also has to approve modifications to the OpenGL API and defines conformance tests. Further details are given in the book OpenGL programming guide by D. Shreiner, M. Woo, and J. Neider [SWN05].

2.5.2   DirectX

Despite the existence of OpenGL implementations for their operating systems, Microsoft developed an alternative graphics rendering API focusing on game and media support for MS Windows, called DirectX[27]. Like OpenGL, DirectX is a hardware independent API to 2D and 3D graphics hardware. DirectX includes the following APIs:

- *DirectSound:* DirectSound supports hardware accelerated 2D or 3D waveform based sound output. This can be used to access 3D capable sound devices.

- *DirectMusic:* DirectMusic is an interface to hardware or software based MIDI sound devices.

- *DirectInput:* DirectInput provides the event handling for input devices, such as mouse, keyboard, or joystick that are connected via supported hardware interfaces (USB, PS/2, or the game port).

- *DirectDraw:* DirectDraw implements hardware based 2D graphics acceleration.

- *Direct3D:* Direct3D implements hardware based 3D graphics acceleration.

- *DirectPlay:* DirectPlay implements a networking interface for the IPX or TCP/IP protocol via network interface cards, modems, or serial connections. It also features a network based voice chat interface for team communication in internet games.

DirectX is distributed as one monolithic software package and is only available for MS Windows based operating systems, on which it is used as the default 3D rendering API.

---

[27]http://www.microsoft.com/directx/ [Accessed 22 February 2006]

2.6 Related client-sided markup and programming languages

Related client-sided markup and programming languages are used to overcome given limitations of a 3D modeling language or data formats. In many of the 3D data formats described above, it is either impossible or time-consuming to implement computationally advanced simulation models or multimedia synchronization. In this section, HTML, ECMAScript, VB Script, and Java are described because of their affinity to web-based implementations.

2.6.1 HTML, ECMAScript, VBScript

Based on an SGML DTD (Standard Generalized Markup Language Document Type Definition), HTML (HyperText Markup Language) documents are plain text documents containing elements that are marked by tags, defined in the HTML standard[28] by the W3C (World Wide Web Consortium).

HTML files can contain various elements such as plain and formatted text, linked images or hyperlinks. A web browser is used to display an HTML document. The speed and quality of content display depend on the web browser's HTML rendering engine.

The lack of synchronization mechanisms for multimedia content can only be compensated by executing appropriate external applications (plug-ins) to display the content. Generally, using plug-ins has to be considered as proprietary. Yet, they are used due to their high degree of functionality. By using a plug-in, a web-browser can process data other than HTML and extend the limited features of HTML. Usually, plug-ins are integrated by an embedding mechanism.

HTML documents can be either statically stored as files or dynamically created through server or client sided scripting languages. Functions and procedures are not supported by HTML but can be realized by scripting languages (ECMAScript-262, better known as JavaScript). A proprietary scripting language is Visual Basic Script (VBScript) that is only supported by the MS Internet Explorer on Windows-based operating systems. Like ECMAScript, VBScript can also be used to detect installed client-sided plug-ins and capabilities in order to deliver content that is optimized for the software portfolio of the web client.

A major drawback of plug-ins is their dependency on the combination of the operating system, the web browser and the input/output interfaces on the client side. The majority of web browser plug-ins are third party closed sourced products. Due to economical reasons, many plug-ins are available only for the most common operating systems and web browsers. Generally, the use of proprietary plug-ins should be avoided if content can be communicated otherwise. If used, compatibility issues should be considered.

---

[28]http://www.w3.org/MarkUp/ [Accessed 07 January 2003]

2.6.2   Java-based extensions

Java is an object-oriented high level programming language, developed by Sun Microsystems. The Java compiler creates platform independent byte code that can be executed by a Java interpreter. Java is portable, dynamic and very expandable by a rich variety of class libraries [Fla00].

It supports network-based distributed applications. When designing web-based 3D information systems, one should consider two major drawbacks of Java as compared to other high level programming languages, such as C++ or C#: the slow performance of the 2D graphical API and the poor native multimedia support[29]. Its lack of hardware accelerated 3D support can be compensated by using Java3D which is described in Section 2.2.1.

Java code can be executed on both the client and the server side. Java applets or Java WebStart applications can be embedded or hyperlinked in any HTML-based web page for client sided execution offering a user-friendly and standardized way of software distribution. At present, Sun's Java 2 Enterprise Edition (J2EE) is increasingly used to implement middleware (for example, servlets for application servers). On the client side, Java applications are used to carry out complex calculations, to display dynamic 2D content or to implement advanced user interfaces.

An example for an interface is presented in a paper entitled "Tweek: Merging 2D and 3D Interaction in Immersive Environments" by P.L Hartling, A.D. Bierbaum, and C. Cruz-Neira. The authors were motivated to design a middleware tool called Tweek by the idea of supporting 2D interactions in immersive environments with a flexible interface that can be used in various virtual reality systems [HBCN02]. Tweek provides an extensible 2D Java graphical user interface that communicates with VR applications.

2.6.3   Flash

Adobe Systems' (formerly: Macromedia) Flash describes both the integrated development environment (IDE) and the Flash Player. The latter is the virtual machine used to run Flash files. The proprietary Flash technology has become a quasi standard for web-based animation and interaction. It features support for vector and raster graphics, a scripting language (ActionScript), and bidirectional streaming of audio and video. Flash is listed in this chapter for four reasons:

- *Interaction support:* With its scripting language ActionScript, Flash provides a very flexible method to integrate interactivity into image-based techniques. Flash shows a reliable performance with regard to time-critical

---

[29]Even the Java Media Framework (JMF) 2.1.1 does not support common media codecs for streaming video formats, such as the RealVideo or the WindowsMedia codec.

interaction (for example, measurement of a subject's reaction time in milliseconds).

- *Content base:* Many existing web-based 2D animations in the domain of psychological experiments are implemented in Flash. Integrating this content into a virtual museum of psychological key experiments could enrich the museum's content base.

- *Image-based 3D content integration:* With third-party software extensions[30], 3DS data files and animations can be exported to Flash and are visualized as 2D vector graphic animations.

- *Geometry-based content integration:* A proprietary VRML node extension by Parallelgraphics allows to use Flash files as texture files in **MovieTexture** nodes. By this, existing Flash animations may be integrated in native 3D environments.

Hence, the Flash technology is suitable if content already exists in the Flash format and can be integrated cost-effectively or if advanced interactivity is required that can not be provided by other programming or scripting languages.

2.7 Conclusion

We have introduced several rendering techniques and modeling languages for web-based 3D applications and their extensions with regard to a browser-based implementation. The major advantages and disadvantages of geometry and image based modeling and rendering techniques are summarized in Table 2.1. Since they represent an often individual and highly flexible combination of both geometry and image-based techniques, hybrid approaches are not seperately mentioned in the table.

The final design decision depends on the complexity of the model that is to be replicated and the system requirements. While image-based methods offer a cost-effective rapid development and high quality photo-realistic rendering on standard graphics hardware, its inability to visualize occlusion-free geometric 3D objects and its limited variety of interactive events, make this technique a good choice for static visualizations that focus on providing a mere visual impression of a spatial environment.

Geometric modeling and rendering offer native 3D environments with free camera movement and often provide better support for programming and/or scripting languages that allow the implementation of event handling for interaction.

---

[30]For example, Swift3D by Electrinrain is a third-party extension with Flash export filters for the 3ds max modeling tool.

	Geometry-based...	Image-based...
...modeling	⊕ High degree of precision ⊕ Variable level of details ⊕ Control of hidden surfaces ⊕ Object hierarchy ⊕ Object-related event handling ⊖ Expensive	⊕ Fast development (rapid prototyping) ⊖ Hidden surfaces ⊖ Resolution dependent ⊖ Data size
...rendering	⊕ Free choice of viewpoint (unless prerendered) ⊖ Rendering time depends on (local) scene complexity ⊖ Advanced graphics hardware required for high quality rendering	⊕ Rendering time independent of scene complexity ⊕ Modest graphics hardware required ⊕ Photo-realistic quality ⊖ Fixed resolution ⊖ Limited amount of viewpoints

Table 2.1: Comparison of geometry-based and image-based modeling and rendering

The major drawbacks are the expensive development costs and the renderer's advanced graphics hardware requirements.

Hybrid methods should be considered. Geometric rendering software manufacturers tend to provide or plan to implement proprietary support for image-based data formats or techniques (for example, movie textures, bump mapping), which allows a better combination of the described methods. On the other hand, some image-based products provide basic support for geometric models (for example, Adobe Atmosphere[31]) or advanced multimedia animations (for example, Macromedia Flash).

Having given an overview of web-based 3D techniques and exemplary applications, we proceed with the definition of an extended concept for a virtual museum and a modeling pipeline for replicated virtual laboratories. For the implementation process, any of the above mentioned techniques can be considered.

---

[31]First released in 2003, Adobe discontinued the Atmosphere product line in 2005.

Chapter 3

Toward a virtual museum for replicated scientific laboratories and experiments

3.1 Introduction

Modeling virtual replications of scientific laboratories and classical experiments is a complex task that covers various research fields such as museology, virtual environments, simulation, and education. There is abundant literature on each of the several aspects.

In this chapter, an extended definition of a virtual museum for replicated historical laboratories and experiments is given. Then, a modeling pipeline for the design of replicated of classical psychological experiments is developed. Thereafter, the metaphorical design of a framework that holds these replicated laboratories is presented with a focus on its conceptual and temporal metaphors. Finally, a structure model for a virtual environment for replicated laboratories is deduced from a similar model for virtual museums.

Due to the primary focus on virtual museums and classical (that is, historical) content, we will first discuss virtual museums and digital heritage.

3.2 Redefining the virtual museum

3.2.1 Virtual museum - a common definition

According to the statutes of the International Council of Museums (ICOM), a museum is defined as

> "[...] a non-profit making, permanent institution in the service of society and of its development, and open to the public, which ac-

quires, conserves, researches, communicates and exhibits, for purposes
of study, education and enjoyment, material evidence of people and
their environment."[ICO01, Art.2, par.1]

In 2001, the ICOM expanded this definition to include "cultural centres and other
entities that facilitate the preservation, continuation and management of tangible
or intangible heritage resources (living heritage and digital creative activity)". Although this amendment vaguely covered digital action, the term 'virtual museum'
remained unreferenced.

As C. Karp points out in his article "Digitising Identity: The Museum Community Meets the Net", the term 'virtual museum' is used in a different context
among the museum and the Internet community [Kar04]. While the term is often
used to express the digital projection of the activities related to a traditional
"bricks-and-mortar" museum (and implying the existence of the same) among
the traditional museum community, the Internet community refers to it as the
digital presentation of heritage material regardless of its affinity to practices of
traditional heritage management institutions.

In 2000, the Internet Corporation for Assigned Names and Numbers (ICANN)
selected seven proposals for new top-level domains, including .museum, which
reflects the particular interest of the Internet community in the heritage management sector. Although this offered a chance to develop a unified definition, a
compromise was made instead. The .museum domain policy statement is based
on the ICOM definition of a museum but distinguishes between "entities that
conduct qualifying activity in born-digital contexts but do not operate physical
museums" and "physical museums that also operate digital museums". It is noteworthy, that the term 'virtual museum' does not appear in the policy but that it
explicitly includes digital-only museums.

In his article "The Development of the Virtual Museum", Schweibenz points out
that the term 'virtual museum' lacks a "generally accepted definition". Four hierarchical categories of web-based museums are identified that define the 'virtual
museum'[Sch04]:

- The *brochure museum* that contains basic information about the real museum and tends to inform potential visitors.

- The *content museum* that provides an object-oriented presentation of the
  museum's collection and lets the virtual visitor explore the objects in a web
  browser. The content is "basically identical" with the collection database
  and is not didactically enhanced.

- The *learning museum* which offers different access points to its virtual visitors according to their profile (age and background knowledge). The site is
  didactically enhanced, information is presented in a content-oriented way,

and hyperlinks to additional information are supposed to improve the virtual visitor's contextual knowledge on a subject.

- The *virtual museum* that - in addition to the content-oriented and contextualized presentation of the institution's collection covered by the learning museum - offers links to other (internal or external) digital collections.

Schweibenz postulates the "memory institution" which combines the digital surrogates from archives, libraries, and museums into one institution that allows a long-term preservation of the digitized content and the access to it.

3.2.2   Virtual heritage

Article 1 of the United Nations Educational, Scientific, and Cultural Organization's (UNESCO) charter on the Preservation of the Digital Heritage states:

> "The digital heritage consists of unique resources of human knowledge and expression. It embraces cultural, educational, scientific and administrative resources, as well as technical, legal, medical and other kinds of information created digitally, or converted into digital form from existing analogue resources. Where resources are *born digital*, there is no other format but the digital object. Digital materials include texts, databases, still and moving images, audio, graphics, software and web pages, among a wide and growing range of formats. They are frequently ephemeral, and require purposeful production, maintenance and management to be retained. Many of these resources have lasting value and significance, and therefore constitute a heritage that should be protected and preserved for current and future generations. This ever-growing heritage may exist in any language, in any part of the world, and in any area of human knowledge or expression."
> [UNE03]

According to this definition, virtual (that is, digital) replications of experiments, that had a strong impact on the development of a scientific research field, represent digital heritage. This includes experiments that mark historically important methodical or cognitive improvements in scientific research and contribute substantially to the history of a science or a research field.

In the case of psychology, it was, on the one hand, the introduction of a strict scientific research methodology, especially during the late 19th century, that contributed to the development from Wilhelm Wundt's first institute for experimental psychology to the science *psychology* as it is known today. On the other hand, the scientific results acquired by this methodology were substantial and fundamental in the history of psychology.

The aspects concerning preservation and accessibility mentioned in Art. 1 of the charter refer to the general functional demands of long-term data consistency and open access in a digital heritage information system.

Summarizing, digital reproductions of *key* experiments, including psychological key experiments, are digital heritage.

3.2.3   Digital interpretation

A crucial question in the context of digital heritage museums, and virtual exhibitions of replicated historical laboratories alike, is interpretation: By what means can the visitor interpret the historical relevance or the scientific impact of an exhibition object?

As K.H. Veltman points out in his publication "Frontiers of Digital Interpretation", the term *digital interpretation* is used in various contexts in the museum domain [Vel02]. According to the author, it can refer to:

1. Identification of objects in the physical world.

2. Restoration of objects in the physical world (for example, simulation before intervention).

3. Reconstruction of objects in the physical world which are now in ruins or no longer exist.

4. Identification of conventional subjects.

5. Identification of meaning and gestalt constituting the world of symbolic values.

Veltman criticizes that in

> "computer science one finds the assumption that interpretation is a purely mechanical process of feature extraction, which can be nearly and perhaps even completely automated" [Vel02, p.3].

There are abundant applications of pattern recognition algorithms for physical object identification that use automated feature extraction for indexing digital media collections, especially large image collections. Nonetheless, for the scope of this work we will focus on the definitions 2 to 5, describe them with regard to virtual exhibitions, and summarize them in a computer scientific terminology.

As Veltman states, the restoration of historical objects in the real world is based on an interpretation by a conservator or restorer that results in an (often) irreversible intervention in an original object. Due to the possible impact of these actions, physical access to the historical object is only allowed to experts. Even then, experts use virtual simulations, including 3D visualizations, before the restoration process to reduce the risk of damaging the original objects ("simulation before intervention").

Digital interpretations, as virtual ("electronic") reconstructions, are placed in a spatio-temporal context and deduced from various sources ("evidence"). These sources may include movies, photos, paintings, sketches, drawings, maps, and descriptions in books and manuscripts. In digitized form, they are hyperlinked to the reconstructed object's visualization to provide additional context-related information and help the visitor to comprehend the digital interpretation.

Finally, Veltman highlights the importance of providing hyperlinked resources with cultural, religious, and historical knowledge to support the visitor in both the identification of conventional subjects and their symbolic interpretation, with a strong focus on art exhibition. The advantage of providing this information in different multimedia formats for different perceptual channels and user groups is also mentioned.

Hence, Veltman's definitions of *digital interpretation* with regard to virtual museums can be summarized, in IT terminology, as:

- The interactive and reversible virtual simulation and visualization of restoration activities, reserved for restoration experts.

- A collection of multimedia documents or a knowledge database that is accessed by direct interaction with the virtual exhibition object.

We can now proceed to deduce an extended definition of the virtual museum that heeds the demands of the preceding definitions but also incorporates aspects from the computer sciences.

3.2.4 Toward an extended concept of a virtual museum

An extended definition of a virtual museum can be deduced from several aspects. While some definitions state that a virtual museum requires the existence of a real non-digital museum, others allow digital-only virtual museums. The aforementioned .*museum* TLD policy includes both forms in a definition that distinguishes exclusively between them. As S. Dietz *et al.* point out in their publication "Virtual Museum (of Canada): The Next Generation",

> "[s]uch existing definitions present a number of binaries: the physical and virtual versus the virtual only; the virtual of physical and the virtual of born digital; being connected online versus connected in a specific physical space." [DBB+04]

The authors express that this differentiation is irrelevant for a definition. Likewise, we consider a virtual museum to be any arbitrary re-combination of the mentioned representations that are not necessarily exclusive of each other.

Interactivity

In contemporary exhibitions, we can identify two basic types of interactivity:

1. Implicit object interactivity is given if an exhibited object is *per se* interactive, regardless of any additional information resources. For example, numerous modern art installations are inherently interactive as they either allow or even require visitor interaction. The same applies to many objects in the domain of digital media art.

2. Informational object interaction is given if an object features interactivity as a means for providing digital interpretation, that is, context-related digital information.

Unlike art objects, historical technical (re-)constructions, as they can be found in technical museums, are often *per se* interactive and provide information (in both the real and the virtual world) by allowing the visitor to interact with them. Here, knowledge is created if a visitor understands an object's construction design, its mode of operation, and its functionality through immediate interaction with the object. Hence, digital interpretation is not limited to hyperlinking interactive object parts to information resources, as Veltman states, and we can extend *digital interpretation* by interpretation results that can be gained through direct user interaction with the virtual object.

Reversibility

In the real world, art, historical, and technical objects are often not intended for direct interaction or long-term exhibition to human visitors, due to the danger of causing irreversible damage. Art objects can be irreversibly damaged by contact with extensive amounts of light or ultraviolet radiation (for example, flashlight, sunlight) or chemical materials (for example, substances emitted by human visitors). While the exhibition of rare and sensitive art exhibits with appropriate safety measures still forms a common compromise between reducing the risk of irreversible damage and the delivery of museum services for the public, most technical objects allow or even require interactivity to demonstrate their functionality. Nonetheless, technical machinery is often designed to be operated by experts. Abnormal operation may cause irreversible damage or destroy an asset. Assuming a technical asset is operated correctly, it still is subject to abrasion and requires permanent maintenance. The potential risk of irreversibly damaging exhibits through visitor interaction is crucial in real world exhibitions.

Simulation

With regard to the user group, we have to discuss why, as Veltman states, interactive simulation techniques and 3D visualization for digital interpretation should be reserved to experts. If virtual simulations facilitate the interpretation of a digitized object by visualizing an interactive process between visitor/user and the object, reversible simulations are an important means of digital interpretation, not only for experts. It is irrelevant whether or not users of the simulation carry out irreversible actions afterwards, in the real world. Unlike with exhibits in the real world, visitors can use simulations to plan, conduct, and interpret "what-if"-scenarios without endangering heritage or expensive collections and use this means of digital interpretation for knowledge creation. Reversible simulation by means of virtual reproductions and simulations offers new possibilities for the presentation of sensitive or interactive exhibits.

Therefore, a virtual museum dedicated to replicated historical laboratories and scientific experiments can be defined. Its content belongs to the scientific or technical domain and represents digital heritage, if key experiments are involved. The "exhibits" are complex interactive sets of objects that are composed of

1. A visual model acquired by geometric, image, or hybrid modeling techniques that visualize the experimental equipment and other context-related objects,

2. An interaction model with a focus on direct object interaction, and/or a simulation model that heeds reversibility aspects, both of which are based on a formal numerical, stochastic, or logical model description.

The existence of a non-digital exhibit or museum is not required.

Due to the complexity of creating a model that heeds spatial, interaction, and simulation aspects, a modeling pipeline for the creation of virtual laboratories is required, which is specified in the following section. Thereafter, metaphorical design questions arise, as "rooms" have to be aligned as exhibits in a virtual museum environment.

3.3 Virtual laboratory modeling pipeline

In this section, a synthesis model for the replication of virtual laboratory experiments is proposed that covers both historical and non-historical experiments with regard to required assets, reversibility, interaction, and simulation related aspects. Each virtually replicated experiment represents an exhibition object for a virtual museum of replicated laboratories.

The modeling process focuses on the creation of a virtual environment composed by a navigable world and built using adequate modeling languages, dynamic scene objects, and acting characters. Scenic objects are preferentially modeled in 3D and characterized by graphic and acoustic attributes; character's, animal's, or object's actions are based on deterministic and non-deterministic plans or behavior, as in an interactive hyperstory. The user explores the virtual world by watching the experiments and interacting with appropriate interfaces and immediately obtains feedback. The complete modeling pipeline is depicted in Figure 3.1. The conceptual design, the conceptual and perceptual model, and interfaces are its main aspects that are discussed and explained in the following subsections.

3.3.1   Conceptual design

Before starting the modeling process and the asset acquisition, the modeling technique must be determined with regard to the target platform, constraints, budget and available resources.

The decision that leads to a system's conceptual design should be discussed under various aspects. From the user's perspective, the decision whether to use a 2D or 3D model depends on the type of the experiment. In a paper entitled "Virtual Galleries: Is 3D better?", Z. Hendricks, J. Tangkuampien, and K. Malan report on virtual African art galleries [HTM03]. In a comparative study, 2D and 3D environments were evaluated. The results of the user study showed that users have a clear preference for 3D environments only if they are not too complex and provide the users with a high level of navigational support. While there are many effective visualization methods for large amount of information in both 2D and 3D form, 2D settings are better suited to convey huge amount of information that exists in sequential form.

In addition to this user-centred aspect, we present two taxonomies: one is based on the level of realism and the other is based on the complexity of the geometric model. Thereafter, we conclude content-based design requirements with regard to (historical and non-historical) psychological experiments.

3.3.1.1   Taxonomy "Level of Realism"

In their article "On architectural design in virtual environments", H.A. Bridges and D. Charitos [BC97b] classify virtual environments (VE) by their levels of realism:

- *Hyperrealities*: VEs that tend to represent the complexity of the real world.

- *Selective realities:* VEs that give a more simplified overall representation by applying a different level of realism for each asset of the real environment. Selective realities offer a way to represent information according to its relevance. Selected assets are represented with a high degree of realism, others are shown with less detail and still others are not included at all.

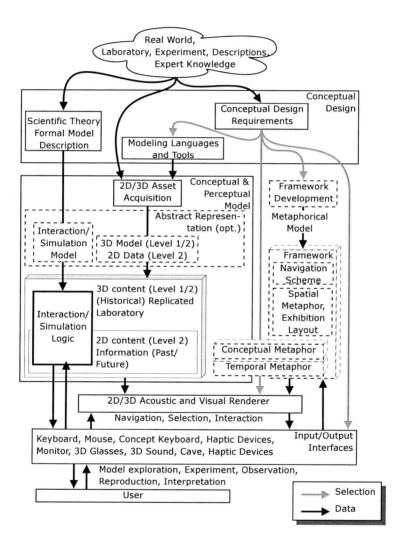

Figure 3.1: Model synthesis for replicated virtual laboratories

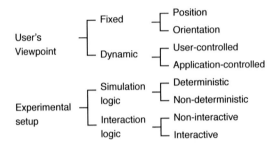

Figure 3.2: Taxonomy "User/Experiment"

- *Abstractions:* VEs that contain either abstract information about complex real environments or information that cannot have a physical representation.

For both geometric and image-based modeling, it can be summarized that this taxonomy corresponds to a budgetary taxonomy: The production of hyperrealities has to be considered as more expensive than selective realities or abstractions.

3.3.1.2 Taxonomy "User/Experiment"

We can define another taxonomy of virtual laboratory environments with regard to the user's viewpoint and the complexity of the experimental setup (see Figure 3.2).

It is important to note that, due to the nature of the web-based modeling and rendering techniques described in Chapter 2, this taxonomy can also be used to deduce applicable software techniques. While IBR is mainly used for fixed user viewpoints, geometry-based techniques (either in navigable or prerendered worlds) are usually used with dynamic user viewpoints. Furthermore, interactivity requires event handling and a complex simulation logic may require an implementation in a higher programming language.

3.3.1.3 Virtual laboratory conceptual design requirements

With regard to the taxonomies given above, we can now conclude content-related requirements for the conceptual design of virtual laboratory environments. At least seven major requirements should be considered for the determination of a suitable modeling technique. While all seven requirements apply to the 3D replication of a historical laboratory, requirements 2 through 7 apply to general (that is, to both historical and non-historical) 3D replications of laboratories:

1. **Historical context representation**: Presenting the historical context in which an experiment was originally carried out is a crucial aspect of historical laboratories. The user should learn under which conditions these experiments were carried out and apprehend their often provisional nature. While - except for cases involving implicit 3D experiments - 2D models are sufficient to represent an abstract model of an experiment, they lack visualization of the laboratory's historical spatial environment. Information about the historical context is often abstract. Especially in a 2D model, such information has to be provided separately through additional sources, such as photographs or text descriptions. A 3D model allows the system designer to integrate contextual information in the space surrounding the experiment setup. For example, the provisional nature of Skinner's first test rigs, which he assembled himself on a farm in Pennsylvania, can be emphasized by locating the experimental setup within a 3D room equipped with corresponding tools.

2. **Impact of occluded surfaces**: Surface occlusion can be partial (such that objects cannot be seen from at least one viewpoint) or total (such that objects cannot be seen from any viewpoint). Surface occlusion of objects with crucial functionalities within an experimental setup (that is, these objects are invisible to the user) can disturb the knowledge transfer. In the latter case, 3D implementation must offer sufficient viewpoints or other techniques (for example, surface transparency) to remedy this problem while, at the same time, heeding the demand of historical authenticity.

3. **Implicit 3D experiments**: Experiments that involve implicit 3D setups are best suited for implementation based on geometrical modeling and free real-time user navigation.

4. **Animation complexity**: Animations contained within a laboratory vary in their degree of complexity and may require advanced control logic that implies the use of high-level programming languages. Examples include complex simulations, complex interaction controls, and high-precision numerical computations.

5. **Interaction complexity**: Some experimental setups require complex interaction logic and application programming interfaces to higher programming languages.

6. **I/O Interface requirements**: With regard to the available perception channels, special input/output interface requirements must be defined that allow the user to conduct the experiment.

7. **Data format consistency**: A set of multiple 3D worlds should be implemented in a consistent data format. Although multiple authoring and

modeling tools may be applied, the use of a consistent web-based data format for content delivery often implies commitment to a special modeling technique.

Once the sources have been evaluated according to the requirements, the modeling languages and tools (see Chapter 2), the corresponding visual and acoustic renderering software, and applicable input/output interfaces can be defined. For reasons of consistency, the selected modeling method also affects the design of the framework system that connects the laboratories (see Figure 3.1).

Once the modeling method has been determined, the conceptual and perceptual models can be developed.

3.3.2   The conceptual and perceptual models

The **conceptual model** results from mapping the real or fictitious world situation into a computer model using all digital media, including media types supported by the acoustic and visual renderer [BL02]. With regard to the psychological content, the conceptual model represents an experiment in its historical context focusing primarily on

- Visual (historical and non-historical) 2D/3D assets.

- A formal model description of the underlying scientific theory.

- Representation of the applied scientific methodology.

The **perceptual model** is created by transferring the conceptual model through a set of perceptual channels supported by the system. It can be perceived by the visitor using only those information channels available to him. With the perceptual model, it is important to provide surprising elements to provoke attention in order to enhance the perception process. Often, the resulting graphic outcome is, if we consider rasterized animated sequences, highly complex and is strongly compressed during the reception process. Intuitive correspondences between graphical and aural objects can be defined. Attention must be paid to the fact that only a small number of sounds can be memorized.

3.3.2.1   2D/3D asset acquisition

One of the main tasks during virtual reproduction of a historical experiment or laboratory is 2D/3D asset acquisition. The assets for the conceptual model are developed either from expert knowledge, which provides the theoretical background and a formal model description of the scientific theory and research methodology, through descriptions from authentic sources or from existing (virtual and real) laboratory visualizations.

If an asset that is to be virtually replicated does not physically exist, it has to be modeled from descriptions or visualizations given in authentic sources using software as mentioned in Chapter 2.

If an original space, place, scene, or set of assets physically exists, the virtual assets can be generated by various manual or automated methods, including manual 3D geometric reconstruction/modeling, laser scanning, and photogrammetry, depending on whether geometry or image-based techniques or hybrid approaches are used in the final implementation (see Chapter 2).

We define two content implementation levels. The first level (**Level 1 content**) describes the modeling of a 3D historical key experiment, its 3D assets, and its simulation and interaction model with a focus on 3D and historical content. At least one level 1 content type *experiment* per historical present is mandatory. In fact, the system is designed to visualize one historical *key* experiment per historical present. However, any experiment that is known to need results from more than one test group or user group[1] may require two or more different implementations, each of which may require different acoustic and visual models, simulation models, perception channels, or interaction facilities, respectively. At runtime, only one of them is visualized, depending on the user's choice or a distribution algorithm that automatically assigns visitors to test groups according to the experiment's design.

The second level (**Level 2 content**) describes optional content that covers additional preceding and succeeding 2D or 3D experiment and related multimedia documents in order to heed the didactic requirements (see Section 3.2.1) by presenting the key experiment in a historical context, including extensions of the key experiments or experiments that are based on the same scientific theory. Level 2 content focuses on the contextual representation of the historical key experiment.

3.3.2.2 Interaction/simulation model

The interaction model and the simulation model help to visualize the theoretical background and the research method by providing the following functionalities:

- *Interactivity,* which allows the visitor to interact with central objects in the experimental setup in correspondence with the theory and the (historical) research methodology of the experiment.

- *Reversibility,* which allows the visitor to start or re-create the experiment from arbitrary time positions.

- *Parameterized simulations,* which allow the visitor to conduct an experiment with different configurations.

---

[1]Although the Replicave system supports this feature, it was not required for the currently implemented experiments.

Although both the interaction and simulation model may be defined in a single model, they are listed separately with regard to their implementation. While event routing for interactivity is often supported by 3D modeling languages, complex simulations may require higher programming languages.

The **simulation model** focuses on visual animation sequences that, in a given interaction-free time interval, are generated autonomously. For example, the process of monitoring the behavior of a rat in a box without any interaction requires an autonomous simulation model that controls the rat's movements and actions. The **interaction model** focuses on providing the user with sufficient interactivity based on event monitoring and handling. Both models are important for the visualization of reversible experimental models.

When modeling a psychological experiment, the nature of the experiment should be examined first, in order to develop a basic model, which can be refined later. In the psychological encyclopedia *Lexikon der Psychologie*, H.-P. Musahl defines the term *experiment* as follows:

> "*Ein Experiment ist ein willkürlicher Eingriff in einen 'natürlichen Ablauf', der planmäßig, kontrolliert und erwartungsgerichtet definierte Bedingungskonstellationen mit dem Ziel herbeiführt, die Folgen dieses Eingriffs möglichst umfassend zu beobachten.*[2]"[Mus00a]

The author points out that an experiment preliminary postulates that a given situation is characterized by a sequence of events ('natural process') based on causality, that is, the concept of cause and effect. In contrast to the mere observation of a natural process, an experiment allows to intentionally (**'arbitrariness'**) and methodically (**'variation of conditions'**) cause events under controlled (**'control'**) and reduced (**'isolation of variables'**) conditions with the intention of a complete (**'completeness of variables'**), exact (**'reliability of measurement'**), and reproducible (**'reproducibility'**) observation.

In the same encyclopedia, the author also defines a taxonomy of experimental methods that can assist model designers to determine the specific type of psychological experiment and to develop an appropriate interaction and simulation model (see Figure 3.3). Compared to the other mentioned experimental methods, the "lab experiment" features the highest degree of internal validity with regard to the experimental outcome and offers a fundamentally scientific method for the research of causal relationships.

With regard to the experimental setup and the technical feasibility of an implementation, the user's role as a subject, historical researcher, or mere observer must be determined. If an experiment that is to be replicated tends to result in an infeasible implementation, alternative user roles or partial replications that

---

[2] "An experiment is an arbitrary intervention in a 'natural process' that effectuates defined combinations of conditions in a methodical, controlled, and expectation-oriented manner, with the intention to scrutinize the results of this intervention."

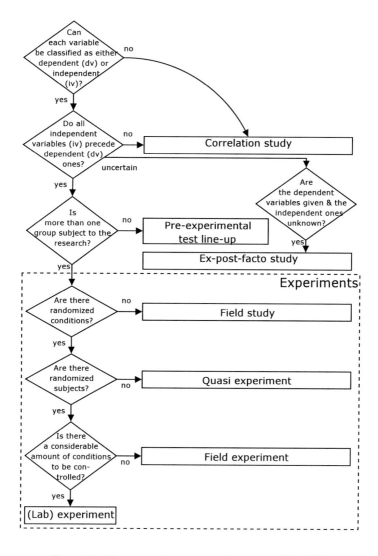

Figure 3.3: Taxonomy of experimental methods [Mus00b].

reflect the applied methodology should be considered. Furthermore, this may include a restriction of the interaction or simulation model's parameters, with regard to the implementation's feasibility or in order to focus on special aspects of an experiment, instead of the complete setup.

Complex simulation models for psychological experiments are often based on non-deterministic mathematical models, such as Markov models, statistical models, and neuronal models and simulate the behavior of an animal or human subject during an experiment with a given set of input parameters in order to reproduce output data that reflects the underlying psychological theory. In addition, they allow the visualization of other dynamic objects, including complex scientific instruments, to underline the scientific methodology.

3.3.2.3   Abstract representation

The abstract representation describes the optional process of mapping the conceptual, perceptual, interaction, or simulation model into a software-based design model or model description from which an implementation can be deduced. The abstract representation consists of digital data that may require further processing in order to be deployed in a functional information system. This data can include, in arbitrary data formats, a written storyboard or hyperstory, 2D data (multimedia data), 3D model data (for example, raw data from laser-scanners, complex geometric models from 3D model libraries), or the description of an interaction or simulation model. An abstract representation provides a reliable documentation for complex algorithms and a fall-back if a deployed 3D technique is discontinued or if hardware improvements allow to enhance existing models in terms of quality or quantity.

While 2D data and 3D models are often directly stored in a deployable data format, the interaction and simulation models should, especially in complex scenarios, preferably be designed by utilizing standardized modeling languages, such as the Unified Modeling Language (UML). For example, an experiment can be modeled in UML by use case diagrams, activity diagrams, or interaction diagrams. Depending on the modeling or programming language, the model's complexity and (optionally) available CASE tools, further details can be modeled in class diagrams (preferably for simulation models that are to be implemented in an object-oriented programming language), state diagrams (for example, event handling), sequence/collaboration diagrams (message handling), or other diagram types or UML objects [SvG00]. Instead of UML, simulation models can also be described as mathematical models, such as a Markov model which is defined by a state transition matrix.

3.3.2.4 Interfaces

With regard to the perceptional model, each experiment's implementation must support appropriate input and output interfaces. The output interfaces include visualization devices, such as a 2D color display (monitor) or 3D glasses, 2D or 3D audio devices, and haptic devices (for example, force feedback devices). The default input devices are a keyboard and a mouse. In addition, joysticks, concept keyboards, and special 3D devices, such as a 3D space mouse or a 3D glove, may be supported. However, special devices must be supported by corresponding APIs of the acoustic or visual renderer or by middleware. This also applies to devices for special user groups, such as illiterate users or users with a hearing impairment.

An overview of recent and cost-effective interaction techniques for the exploration of web-based 3D museums and objects contained therein is given in an article by P. Petridis *et al.*, entitled "Exploring and Interacting with Virtual Museums" [PWM⁺05]. In addition to virtual reality visualization techniques, the authors extended their research on augmented reality applications. However, Replicave does not support augmented reality interfaces or visualization.

3.4   Metaphorical design

In this section, the metaphorical design of spatial and temporal metaphors in a virtual museum of replicated laboratories is discussed. As already mentioned in Section 3.3 and illustrated in Figure 3.1, the framework system's 3D modeling technique is predetermined by the laboratories' conceptual design. However, the framework provides an exhibition layout based on a spatial metaphorical framework design with navigation schemes. Content representing scientific theories, corresponding key experiments, and the historical context of the experiments is organized through a temporal and a conceptual metaphor, respectively, which are defined in this section. First, we give an overview of related work on this topic and introduce a terminology.

In a paper entitled "Exploiting the Potential of 3D Navigable Virtual Exhibition Spaces" by C. Cerulli [Cer99], the author is concerned with the definition of the historical and cultural context in which the development of virtual exhibition space needs to be placed. Cerulli proposes a survey throughout the years from the sixteenth century's galleries to contemporary virtual galleries on the Web, where the exhibition space could be a text-based environment, a 2D graphical interface, or a 3D model accessible through the Internet and visualized by digital images, videos, 3D computer models, and virtual sculptures. Important analogies and differences between real and virtual museums are developed. The potential differences are:

- *Absence of physical constraints.* The lack of physical and temporal restrictions involves new exhibition layouts and navigation schemes.

- *Spatio-temporal discontinuity.* The spatial and temporal sequence along the circulation paths of physical places is replaced by a subsequent presentation of information screens accessible by an adequate interface. Navigation is achieved by hyperlinks. Jumps between objects or environments that are spatially or temporally non-contiguous but contain related information can help enlarge the horizon of the user.

- *Scale.* The scale of the environment can be altered which allows almost arbitrary zoom levels.

A museum without walls (that is, without a continuous boundary between gallery and non-gallery space) is postulated. However, this may hinder the perception of spatial and temporal concepts generally acquired by the direct experience of the environed design by moving actively on coherent paths with clear navigational decisions.

Therefore, modern modeling languages provide different levels of detail and an efficient collision control. Thus, if wanted, the navigation can be reduced to meaningful movements between juxtaposed objects with a real sensation of distance. Metaphors like elevators, thresholds or intersection spaces can provide temporal coherence.

While many real or virtual exhibitions usually focus on exhibiting individual static objects (for example, art or historical exhibitions), the exhibition of replicated laboratories requires a more distinctive definition of the term *object.* Here, the exhibited *object* is an entire room, thus, an architectural space with physical constraints that consists of a set of objects. As such, each laboratory room is accessible through at least one entrance, a threshold, and is located along a navigational path.

In a paper by Fei Li and Mary Lou Maher, entitled "Representing Virtual Places - A Design Model for Metaphorical Design" [LM00], the authors are concerned with the representation and design of virtual worlds that both create a sense of place and also include an awareness of others in the place. Based on a model given by Lakoff and Johnson [LJ80, LJ99] they present three structures of the cognitive unconscious that provide the basis for understanding how metaphors influence our ability to make sense of subjective experience. Our experiences show that the metaphorical reference to physical places must be completed by a reference to the time scale.

The metaphorical design includes the following four concepts:

- Basic level concepts that describe a basic understanding of objects in the place and their common relations with regard to designing basic categories that allow users interact intuitively with world components.

- Semantic frames defining relationships in the virtual place among whole fields of related concepts and words that express them, filling out the intended use and the behavior of the place with a consistent set of properties and actions.

- Spatial-relation concepts allowing the designer to define consistent actions on the virtual objects as the person would expect to do with the corresponding physical objects. This aspect is related to navigation.

- Time-relation concepts giving meaningful representation of the time scale in the virtual place using metaphors to move in time. They allow time-consistency of objects in the virtual place.

As illustrated in Figure 3.1, the exhibition of multiple experiments in a virtual museum requires a framework system based on a metaphorical model. A spatial metaphor is defined that implies an exhibition layout and a navigation scheme. In designing and understanding virtual worlds, creating a place that is consistent with our understanding of the physical world will allow us to consistently apply the primary metaphors we used. Due to the nature of the exhibition objects (that is, laboratory rooms), a building with continuous boundaries was chosen as the primary framework metaphor.

Experiments that represent the same scientific theory are connected through a contextual metaphor. The different historical key experiments represent historical presents and are, therefore, connected through a temporal metaphor.

Figure 3.4 gives a graphical representation of the spatio-temporal metaphorical design of the building with an access hall, a gallery assembling curricula vitae of psychologists, a media lab with collected works, a video presentation, and pictures, and different floors for each key experiment. The historical present is reached through an elevator (temporal metaphor), which gives the opportunity to load the corresponding world. In addition to the key experiment, the user optionally explores the past and future relative to the actual époque by walking in a floor (contextual metaphor) and opening doors to related experiments.

In Cerulli's above mentioned paper [Cer99], the author also summarizes a taxonomy of generic space-establishing elements in virtual environments, based on a model given by Bridges and Charitos [BC97b], that defines the virtual environment as a closed system that consists of solid and void spatial elements that are framed to form the virtual environment. The solid space-establishing elements, called *props*, are classified by their form (2D or 3D objects) and function. With regard to their function, they can be divided into bounding objects (defining a space boundary) and landmark objects (serving as a point of reference).

The void spatial elements, called *sets*, are divided into four types:

- *Places* are the spaces where activities are carried out. They are defined by their boundaries and should follow a design that allows the user to discern its "inside" and "outside" as well as the activities that take place in it.

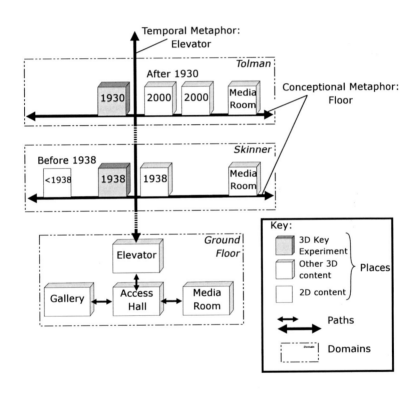

Figure 3.4: Metaphorical design

- *Paths* imply dynamic action and consist of a starting and an end point and an evident direction to follow.

- *Domains* "can rather be seen as a mental abstraction of the environment experienced by the subject through paths and places"[Cer99]. For each participant, an environment is organized into domains, defined by paths and places.

- *Thresholds* are "transitions or intersection spaces between any other spatial element" [Cer99]. As such, they are crucial locations for the navigation within the virtual environment.

Bridges and Charitos consider architectural design "as one of the disciplines, which may contribute to the design of virtual environments" [BC97b, pp.144-145]. Their proposed design methods are influenced by an architectural design background but not limited to it. Although the usage of a building metaphor for the framework system would allow a strict focus on architectural design, we will refer to the above mentioned terminology, as proposed by Bridges and Charitos, to deduce the design of the temporal and the conceptual metaphor.

3.4.1   Temporal metaphor

Each (level 1) key experiment represents a unique historical present defined by the name of the theory, the name of the person who founded that theory, and the year of its foundation. For convenience, the real present is also defined as a special case of a historical present. Hence, the temporal metaphor allows the user to change from one historical present to another. This implies that is has to be accessible from each historical present. Its layout and complexity depend on the total amount of historical presents that are available within the system.

The maximal amount of paths to connect n given historical presents with unique thresholds that directly lead the user from one historical present to another is $\sum_{i=1}^{n} i = \frac{n(n+1)}{2}$. This is equivalent to the total amount of edges in a fully meshed graph with n vertices with edges representing paths and vertices representing thresholds, respectively. The advantage of a fully meshed design is the direct connection between the place of departure and the destination which may reduce the transfer time to a minimum. Nonetheless, the amount of required paths increases at a quadratic rate which may entail subsequent and complex layout changes in all existing historical present modules whenever a historical present is added to or removed from the system. Depending on the layout and the metaphors, the volumetric size requirement of additional paths may counteract a potentially compact layout and may even result in longer transfer times.

The minimal amount of paths for a vertical connector with n thresholds is $n - 1$. An exemplary layout is a building with $n - 1$ individual staircases that connect all adjacent n levels of the building from the bottom to the top. In the worst case, a visitor would have pass all $n-1$ staircases to get from the ground to the top floor.

Summarizing, the design decision for a temporal connector depends on various conditions. If the system contains a variable amount of historical presents, the temporal connector should be generated dynamically to avoid high maintenance costs for static models. Depending on the amount of space available, the thresholds should be designed and sized in accordance with the metaphorical and spatial design of their environment. Finally, the path design and layout should metaphorically comply with the environment and reflect a compromise between the demand of short distances and the required volumetric space. The volumetric space requirement can be limited by superposing paths: One or more paths are fully or partially overlaid at identical spatial locations and form a *metapath*. However, this implies that the user is still able to navigate from the origin to the destination.

Finally, we can define an active and a passive path navigation in order to reduce the volumetric requirements. In *active path navigation*, the user navigates freely and deliberately along a path within a global coordinate system. In *passive path navigation*, the user's avatar is encapsulated in a bounding box with a local coordinate system while the bounding box and the user's avatar are transported along a pre-defined path toward the destination threshold. Although the bounding box may be designed as a place, its ability to create a user experience of being moved between thresholds provides it with a path property.

3.4.2 Conceptual metaphor

The main functionality of the conceptual metaphor is the visualization of paths and thresholds that allow the user to navigate to the key (level 1) experiment and, optionally, to other preceding or subsequent (level 2) experiments related to the key experiment or its central scientific theory, by aligning the experiments in a logical order. Depending on the system-wide metaphorical concept, the visualization of places may also be required.

The spatial alignment of the paths leading toward the laboratory thresholds should follow an order that is best suited pedagogically which is not necessarily a chronological order. The alignment is to be deduced from expert knowledge, especially from didactical sources about the scientific topic.

Another layout property is the conditional accessibility of an experiment. The administrator has to decide whether or not access restrictions to any of the implemented experiments of a group are to be applied for pedagogical or statistical reasons. Access restrictions may apply if an experiment is implemented with both an experimental group and a control group. Here, the amount of users participating in each group should be evenly balanced, which defines a condition.

For systems with dynamic content, a dynamic layout and spatial alignment of paths and thresholds is required. Otherwise, statically modeled layouts have to be adapted manually. Conditional accessibility generally implies a dynamically generated metaphor visualization.

To allow the user to navigate toward a laboratory, an appropriate description of each threshold is required. It should, at least, contain a text description of the experiment. Additional information, such as the scientist's name and the year of its origin, is a recommended option.

3.5 A structure model of a virtual environment for replicated laboratories

The design of a structure model of a virtual environment for replicated laboratories, as proposed in this section, is deduced from a model for virtual museums. With regard to presentation, conservation, and education, replicated virtual laboratories are interpreted as heritage and museum objects.

In a paper entitled "Toward the Synchronized Experiences between Real and Virtual Museum" Yong-Moo Kwon *et al.* propose a model of a virtual museum by defining real and virtual museum services, grouping them in the three logical layers *inspection, research and communication,* and *documentation and storage,* and synchronizing both real and virtual museum services [KHL+03]. The virtual museum services are *immersive experience, 4D content explorer*[3], *innovative inquiry, interactive annotation,* and XML-based databases while the real museum services are represented by the services *exhibition, education and communication,* and *acquirement and conservation.*

The deduction of a new model for an exhibition of replicated virtual laboratories is realized by analyzing each real and virtual service of the original model and applying it as a replicated lab service with optional modifications to the individual service's functionalities. The complete structure model of a virtual environment for replicated laboratories in given in Figure 3.5.

Assuming a real museum of replicated historical experiments, the three "real" services correspond to the ones from the real museum and are specified as follows:

- *Exhibition:* This service provides the immersive environment in which all replicated lab assets are exhibited and in which the experimental environment is provided that, optionally, allows the conduction of a given experiment. It also includes the museum's framework system (that is, its architectural layout) and provides navigational paths.

- *Education and communication:* This service represents all aspects of the asset alignment that may help to initiate or sustain a knowledge creation

---

[3]The 4D content explorer is a spatio-temporal visualization tool.

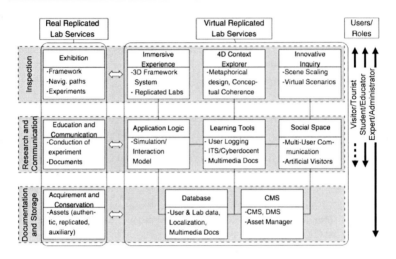

Figure 3.5: The structure model of a virtual environment for replicated laboratories

process and that are related to education or communication. This includes additional multimedia-based information and the visualization of dynamic results and measured data that are generated during the conduction of the experiment.

- *Acquirement and conservation:* This service includes authentic, replicated, or auxiliary assets which represent the complete set of all real objects involved in a replicated laboratory. It provides assets with a temporal attribute. The temporal attribute of original (historical) asset is equal to the date[4] of its historical creation, whereas the temporal attribute of a replicated asset is set to the date of its assumed historical existence. Furthermore, auxiliary assets are included for educational reasons or if original or replicated assets are missing.

In addition to a real museum, the exhibition and availability of historical experiments imply different functionalities for some of the assets and additional roles for the visitor. If an experimental setup defines one or more organic lifeforms as an experimental subject, the visitor can take three roles: If an organic lifeform other than the visitor is the subject of the experiment, the visitor takes the role of either an **investigator** or a **spectator**. In this case, the organic lifeform is an

---

[4]The term *time* refers to a set of time values, at which the existence of an asset is verified or assumed. Normally, but not necessarily, this is a time interval.

asset, that is subject of visual inspection and simultaneously generates scientific data for research. If the visitor is in the **subject**'s role, he temporarily becomes an asset of the experiment himself. Although not necessarily being visible to himself, he may function as a subject of inspection to other visitors, for example in multi-user environments or simply by generating scientific data during the experiment.

Hence, living organisms, that represent assets in an experiment, have two functionalities. As visible objects they belong to the immersive experimental environment that is part of the *exhibition* service located in the *inspection* layer. As objects controlled by biological, physical, or chemical processes they continuously generate discrete data that represents the basic information on which the correctness of a scientific theory can be verified. Representing the scientific theory and communicating an interpretation of the results generated during the conduction of an experiment in accordance with the given theory is the main educational task. Therefore, the control-related asset parts belong to the *conduction of an experiment* functionality located in the *research and communication* layer.

Given the definition of the three services for an (assumed) museum for real replicated laboratories, new virtual "replicated lab" services are defined with regard to a synchronization with the real "replicated lab" services, as defined above.

The inspection layer

In the *inspection* layer, all three services are applicable to a museum of replicated laboratories with marginal functional changes:

- *Immersive experience:* This service includes all user input/output interfaces, that are required to experience the immersive experimental environment.

- *4D content explorer:* This service provides the necessary means for spatio-temporal content exploration by the user. The functionalities describe implementations of the metaphorical design for spatial, temporal, and contextual coherence.

- *Innovative Inquiry:* Innovative inquiry lists methods for data retrieval or additional information visualization by means that cannot be implemented in a real exhibition. Examples may include but are not limited to scene scaling (that is, the user can zoom into the scene at arbitrary zoom levels), object filtering (for example, application of temporal or contextual filters in object visualization), and visualization of experimental results.

The education and communication layer

In the *education and communication* layer, changes are required to represent the educational impact of a dynamic experiment and to meet the characteristic attributes of a virtual learning environment (VLE). There are many over-general and over-specific definitions of a VLE. In a paper entitled "Virtual Learning Environments", Pierre Dillenbourg [Dil00] gives an overview on specific criteria of these environments:

- *Design of the information space.* A web-based VLE is an information space. The information requires a structural design. Furthermore, it has to be organized according to numerous functional requirements of a learning environment, including the usage of information in educational interactions, maintaining information, indicating information sources, and re-usability of information in a changing technical environment.

- *Social space property.* A VLE is a social space. Educational interactions occur in a populated environment. The users are inside the information space. As soon as they "see who else is interested by which information", the information space becomes social.

- *Spatial representation.* The information/social space is explicitly represented. While the representation varies from text to 3D immersive worlds, the main design issue is the structural relationship between the spatial representation and the information space.

- *Student's role as a contributor.* In addition to the active role offered by other constructivist environments, a VLE potentially gives a participant the ability to become a member and contributor of the social and information space.

- *Support for both distance and presential learning.* Virtual learning environments are not restricted to distance education. They also enrich classroom activities.

- *Integration of multiple tools.* As in a physical learning environment, a VLE integrates multiple technical and pedagogical tools to support functions such as information, communication, learning, collaboration, and management.

- *Virtual and physical environments overlap.* Except of a few virtual-only environments designed exclusively for distance education, the majority of virtual learning environments are linked to non-computer-based resources (for example, books), interactions (for example, face-to-face or group discussions), or activities (for example, field trips).

All of Dillenbourg's criteria can be applied to virtual museums or exhibition spaces. In a VLE, as well as in a virtual museum, information is organized in an information space. In both environments, a crucial aspect is the spatial representation and the structural relationship between the spatial representation and the information space, as the physical space does not necessarily match the information space.

In her PhD thesis, Michele Dickey is concerned with the design and implementation of 3D virtual worlds for educational purposes [Dic99]. She provides an analysis of the design requirements and limitations of three well-known 3D virtual world implementations. The work gives insight into several learning environments and present research on how virtual worlds are currently being used for both informal and formal education.

Another educational functionality common to both museums and learning environments is guidance. In an article entitled "From Docent to Cyberdocent: Education and Guidance in the Virtual Museum", W.B. Rayward and M.B. Twidale discuss the concept of the docent function that is derived from the nature of a tutors' or docents' work in a real museum [RT99]. First, the authors analyze the work scope of a human docent in a real museum with regard to social and educational aspects. Then, they define an abstract "docent function", a set of required tasks in order to provide the user with guidance. Finally, they introduce the *Cyberdocent* functionality: a set of possible implementations of docent functions using computing technology that enhances the docent functionalities.

In a paper entitled "Virtual Worlds as Architectural Space: An exploration" by V. Zidarich [Zid02], a discussion on the notions of architecture, space, and place is mirrored with rich references to related work. The author observed that people have turned to virtual spaces and inhabit them in virtual communities with social interactions. It is postulated that individuals and space are independent whereas place is a subjective and individual concept in the cyberworld. Place and time have a very strong relationship. "Places evolve through time, with some features and external appearances related to physical semblance changing or being transformed." [Zid02, p.11]

Therefore, the *education and communication* layer contains the following three virtual services:

- *Learning tools*: The *interactive annotations* service is replaced and extended by *learning tools* which serves as a container for all learning related tools, such as a user log, an intelligent tutoring system (ITS), and access to hyperlinked multimedia documents. The user log functionality offers automatic, semi-automatic, or individual logging of annotations and an appropriate user interface for viewing, editing and administrating log entries. User logging describes both active and passive logging of user events. Log entries and annotations may be used for further instruction-related communication between the user and a tutor or an ITS.

- *Social space*: The *social space* service has been added on the *research and communication* level to meet the social space characteristic of a virtual learning environment. Implementations include *multi-user communication* (that is, multi-user visualization, text chat, or video chat) and *artificial visitors*. Artificial visitors describes the concept of visualizing additional (and physically non-existent) visitors in the VE to overcome the emptiness of virtual spaces that is often criticized by users. For exhibitions, the concept of artificial visitors can be limited to the visualization of usernames or 3D avatars. In advanced implementations, artificial intelligence may be added to allow communication between real and artificial visitors.

- *Application logic:* Interactive virtual lab experiments implicitly contain an application logic that reflect the causal relationship of the corresponding scientific theory by an appropriate interaction and simulation. Hence, the *application logic* service provides the simulation *model* and the interaction *model* of the experimental content. Its implementation allows the individual reproduction of an experiment by the user and helps to communicate the underlying scientific theory and research methods. As such, its primary functionality is to support the learning process. Hence, it is located in the *research and communication* layer and synchronized with the *education and communication* service. Furthermore, the *application logic* service is not located within the *documentation and storage* layer because the validity of a scientific theory is considered as being universally valid and is not part of a cultural heritage. However, their implementation, that is, the simulation *logic* and the interaction *logic* (see Figure 3.1), are stored within the *database* service.

The documentation and storage layer

The *database* service is located in the *documentation and storage* layer. It provides access to the laboratory implementation data (that is, laboratory 2D/3D models and their interaction and simulation logic), user data, localized data, and the context-related multimedia documents. Unlike in the original model by Kwon *et al.*, the database format is not limited to XML, although open, flexible and non-proprietary data formats, such as XML, should be preferred.

Due to the heterogeneous structure of the data, a *content management system* service provides additional document, content, and asset management tools that enhance the functionalities of the *database* service with regard to content administration and roles.

In addition to the mentioned services, three user groups can be identified:

- Visitor/Tourist,
- Student/Educator, and
- Expert/Administrator.

For services that imply the usage of different access levels (for example, the database service), roles can be deduced and defined from the corresponding user groups.

Chapter 4

Implementation

In this chapter, the system's architecture and implementation is discussed and described. First, basic design considerations with regard to the underlying system architecture are discussed. Then, software requirements are defined and its integration within a client/server architecture is presented. Thereafter, the Replicave 3D framework system is described, including its initialization procedure and spatial objects (main hall, gallery, media rooms, and temporal and template-based conceptional metaphors). The last sections cover content management and data storage.

The historical laboratories that represent the system's primary content are discussed separately, in Chapter 5.

For better readability, expressions related to a programming or markup language, such as variable or node names, framesets, functions, and database names are printed in Sans-Serif, while VRML node parameters and database tables are printed in *italic*. File, folder, and path names are printed in `mono-space`; a leading `./` indicates the file's position relative to the Replicave web root directory.

4.1 Design considerations

Analyzing the historical experiments of Ebbinghaus, Skinner, Tolman, Sperling, and Duncker (see Chapter 5) with regard to the taxonomy given in Section 3.3.1.3, the impact of each requirement is identified as follows:

- Authentic context representation: The primary criteria with regard to the content of Replicave is the presentation of psychology as an experimental science by visualizing historical psychological laboratories and the experiments conducted therein, as well as their extensions. The historical experiments of Ebbinghaus, Skinner, Tolman, Sperling, and Duncker represent unique spatial object constellations in their experimental setup and a working environment in which the experiment, first proposed by the respective psychologist, was created and carried out. The visualization has to cover both the experimental setup and its spatial historical context, usually an architectural 3D space, that underlines the often provisional nature of the setups. Examples include Sperling's tachistoscope, Tolman's mazes, Skinner's self-made kymograph and constructions for rats, and the memory experiment carried out by Ebbinghaus in his private house. Hence, the primary objects to be visualized by Replicave are 3D laboratory rooms and 3D objects contained therein.

- Impact of occluded surfaces: Occluded surfaces may occur and negatively affect knowledge transfer in the historical experimental setups of Skinner (Skinnerbox with rat, kymograph) and Duncker (container and objects contained). These experiments require sufficient viewpoints that let the user explore all pedagogically important scene details. The landmark experiment by Steck and Mallot also relies on a sufficient amount of viewpoints that offer an occlusion-free view on landmark objects.

- Implicit 3D experiments: Tolman's experiment on mind maps and its extension by Steck and Mallot on the topic of landmark knowledge implicitly deal with navigational paths in a 3D space. If the user is to take the subject's role in either of these experiments, a 3D implementation is required.

- Animation complexity: All interactive experiments imply a time dependent object visualization. The degree of animation complexity ranges from linearly-interpolated rotations (for example, doors in Tolman's maze experiment) to complex organic motions (for example, rat in Skinner's experiment). In the latter case, a simulation logic, described in a higher programming language, is required to trigger single animation sequences in compliance with the scientific model.

- Interaction complexity: All interactive experiments require an interaction design. This ranges from simple interactive control buttons (for example, change of ratio rate in Skinner's experiment) to complex conditional constrains for user/object and object/object interaction (for example, Duncker experiment).

Due to the focus on 3D rooms (Tolman's experiment) with multiple viewpoints and complex simulations, it was decided to reconstruct the historical laboratories primarily by means of geometric modeling. This technique also allows data export to browsers with free user navigation support and to web-compliant data formats. Support for complex calculations should optionally be given by a high-level programming language. Considering the data formats presented in Chapter 2, image-based approaches suffice for a static reconstruction of laboratory rooms. However, they can not deliver advanced animation and interaction support that is required for the majority of the interactive experiments. Furthermore, due to the missing authentic physical environments of the mentioned laboratories, with the exception of Sperling's experiment, image-based methods would still depend on a 3D-based object reconstruction. Hybrid approaches do not offer sufficient support for web capability (amount of data, availability of client-sided visualization software), animation, and interaction.

A software evaluation of Java3D, X3D, and VRML based browsers showed a poor graphical performance and unpredictable development schedule of Java3D as compared to commercial VRML/X3D browsers. Besides, a Java3D installation requires at least three software packages (see Section 2.2.1) which results in administration costs that do not comply with the project's intention of providing a client platform that is easy to install and maintain. X3D was turned down due to X3D browser issues: unsupported nodes, lack of SAI (Scene Access Interface) support, and stability issues. Furthermore, all evaluated 3D modeling tools lacked X3D data export filters.

Since VRML++ file export is not supported by common 3D graphical modeling tools and due to missing VRML97-to-VRML++ converters to port existing projects or libraries, VRML++ was not chosen for implementation. However, modeling tools with VRML++ support are considered as an option for future projects.

While Shout3D does not offer sufficient interactivity support, Macromedia Shockwave3D browsers showed stability and performance issues.

Summarizing, VRML97 with additional proprietary nodes and EAI support was chosen as the primary modeling and visualization language. Interactivity and animation require event handling and timers, which is supported by VRML97. Complex simulations are supported by ECMAScript and Java (EAI). In addition, some content is still rendered in 2D: multimedia documents that lack an appropriate 3D rendering API for visualization, HTML forms used in the evaluation and content management interface, and experiments that are fully or partially implemented in 2D for technical, legal, or budgetary reasons.

Another advantage of geometric modeling is the free user navigation that enables the user to explore a replicated historical laboratory space by navigating through it and to participate in a real-time virtual experiments either as a spectator or as a subject instead of watching a static prerecorded version of an experiment.

4.2 Software requirements

The Replicave 3D environment can be accessed from clients running the Microsoft operating systems Windows XP SP2 and 2000 SP4 with the following additional software:

- Microsoft Internet Explorer 5.01 (or higher)

- BS Contact VRML renderer by Bitmanagement Software GmbH (Vers. 6.1 or higher; hereafter referred to as the BS VRML-plugin)

- DirectX 9.0 (or higher) - OpenGL is optionally supported

- Real Player by RealNetworks[1]

- Macromedia[2] Flash Player

- Microsoft Java Virtual Machine (see Section 4.2.1)

The BS VRML-plugin and the Microsoft Internet Explorer was the only web/VRML browser combination that displayed dynamically generated VRML files correctly and with full support for movie textures (using Real Player), EAI, and both full screen and windowed display.

Replicave requires the following server sided software products:

- PHP Hypertext Preprocessor[3] (Vers. 4.0.6 or higher)

- A Web server with PHP support

- MySQL database (Vers. 3.23 or higher)

- A Posix-compliant TCP/IP-based server operating system supported by the above mentioned server software products.

The current Replicave server is operated under Linux with an Apache web server, PHP, and MySQL.

4.2.1 Java Virtual Machine

In order to use the EAI with VRML for complex simulations, a Java Virtual Machine (JVM) with EAI and VRML browser support has to be installed on the client. The Microsoft JVM (MSJVM) is the only JVM currently supported by Replicave. However, Java applets can be compiled with the Sun JVM, using the compile option -target 1.1 in Sun's javac compiler.

Following an agreement between Sun Microsystems and Microsoft, software currently including the MSJVM will continue to be retired or replaced by versions not containing the MSJVM[4].

Due to this policy, updating any Microsoft Windows software components that refer to the MSJVM, such as the Internet Explorer, may render a working EAI

---

[1]http://www.real.com/
[2]http://www.macromedia.com/
[3]http://www.php.net/
[4]http://www.microsoft.com/mscorp/java/ [Accessed 20 December 2005]

solution on the client unusable. Contents of Replicave that rely on the EAI, are known to work with version 5.00.3810 of the MSJVM which is stored under ./framework/html/plugins/MSJVM/msjavx86_3810.exe. If, for any reason, the MSJVM is removed from the client, it can be re-installed manually. In some cases of combinations of MS Windows XP and Internet Explorer, the Sun JVM may have to be deactivated in the Internet Explorer's configuration.

4.2.2 Development Software

After evaluating various 3D modeling tools with regard to an intuitive GUI, support of advanced design features (animations, NURBS), reliable VRML97 file import and export filters, stability, and budgetary constraints, the following software products were used for 3D modeling:

- Virtock Technologies Spazz3D: a VRML optimized 3D modeling tool with animation support

- Maxon Cinema 4D XL 7 and Blender: advanced 3D modeling tools. Like similar products, the VRML export filter produced triangularized 3D code resulting in a data overhead for all non-plane 3D objects like cylinders or spheres. The products were chosen for their stability, user interface (Cinema 4D), Python scripting support (Blender), and budgetary considerations.

- Parallelgraphics VRML Pad: a text editor with advanced features including "scene graph" and event routing visualization, VRML syntax highlighting, context-based auto-completion, and detection of unused identifiers for code optimization.

A complete list of development tools is given in Appendix A.1.

4.3 Client/server architecture

Database communication between the client and the database server is commonly implemented by using either a two-tier or three-tier architecture.

A two-tier client/server application architecture describes a direct communication between the client and the server. The application logic and the user interface is located on one computer (Tier1) and the database server on another (Tier2). A potential implementation is a VRML-Browser receiving a 3D world description and an application logic (for example, Java applet/JDBC client) from the web server. The browser visualizes the 3D experiment and a user interface. The application logic is integrated in the EAI, which communicates directly with the database server (see Figure 4.1).

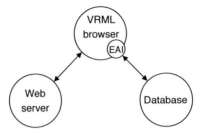

Figure 4.1: A two-tier client/server application architecture

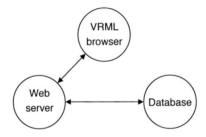

Figure 4.2: A three-tier client/server application architecture

A three-tier client/server application architecture consists of the user interface (Tier1 - client layer), the application logic (Tier2 - server layer) and the database server (Tier3 - database layer). It can be implemented by a VRML-Browser receiving a 3D world description from a web server that includes scripting support and a database connector and which provides the application logic. The architecture is completed by a database server that is controlled by the application logic which resides on the web server (see Figure 4.2).

A three-tier architecture, as described above, was implemented for the following reasons:

- Database connectivity. VRML lacks support for any database connectors. In a two-tier model, an application logic requires Java-EAI techniques based on common database APIs (for example, JDBC). In a three-tier architecture, database access APIs can be implemented on the server side (for example, by using PHP on a web server).

- Security. Leaving the database application logic on the client side in a two-tier approach requires direct access to the database server service for all clients on the internet. This implies a higher security risk as the access is not restricted to a dedicated server as in the three-tier model. Furthermore, deliberate manipulations of the application logic on the client side may result in the generation of falsified data. Implementing the application logic on a dedicated server increases the level of security.

Database access in Replicave is achieved by opening database-related PHP scripts as URLs in the reserved target frame dbscripts (see Figure 4.3).

4.4 System initialization

The database connection parameters (database server, database name, login, password), the default language (see Section 4.4.2), and the initial 3D framework file are defined in the central configuration file ./conf.inc.php.

On opening the URL *http://replicave.informatik.uni-duisburg.de/*, an initial index.html file, located in the Replicave web root folder, is transmitted to the requesting web browser. All client-related access is based on the hypertext transfer protocol (HTTP).

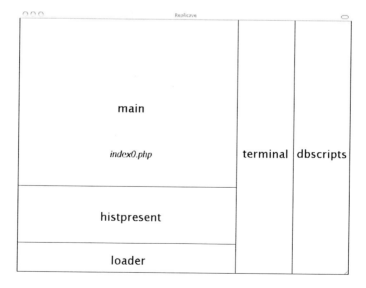

Figure 4.3: Logical HTML frame structure

The `index.html` file defines the HTML frameset TerminalFrames that contains the frameset MainFrame and two additional frames: terminal and dbscripts, both of which are hidden and serve as handlers for PHP-based database communication. The frameset MainFrame contains the three frames main, histpresent, and loader. The main frame is reserved for content display of the 3D framework system, while the histpresent frame is reserved for content display of the conceptual and temporal metaphor, the experiments, and the individual media rooms. The loader frame is hidden and reserved for the `loader.php` script. The logical frame structure is shown in Figure 4.3. Initially, only the main frame is visible in the web browser, all other frames are hidden. On web browsers without HTML frame support, a message is displayed that suggests the use of a frame capable web browser.

4.4.1 Software detection

The file `./html/index0.php` is loaded in the main frame; the other frames are initialized with the resource "about:blank". The `index0.php` file calls several software recognition routines based on ECMAScript[5] and Visual Basic Script to detect the web browser's manufacturer and version number, the VRML plugin(s), and the media player(s) installed on the client computer (see Table 4.1). Each detection routine prints hyperlinks to the corresponding software manufacturer's website. A customized BS Contact manual that is stored in the `./html/doc` folder is also hyperlinked.

The scripts are based on the VRML Plugin and Browser Detector [NIS05] by the NIST (National Institute of Standards and Technology) and have been split into separate files for ease of maintenance and adapted to meet the software prerequisites mentioned in Section 4.2.

If all prerequisites are met on the client PC, a button is displayed that allows the user to enter the 3D environment (see Figure 4.4).

An URL redirection for an automatic launch of the 3D environment after a successful software detection caused stability issues with Microsoft Internet Explorer and was, therefore, not implemented.

For any unmet software requirement, a text is displayed listing the name of the missing software, an URL for its acquisition, and, optionally, a short text-based problem description. Depending on the impact of the missing plugin, the user can still launch the 3D environment manually but is informed that several features may not operate as expected.

---

[5]This requires JavaScript support by the web browser.

File	Task
index0.php	Generation of HTML code in main frame. Display language selector. Storage of user's language selection in session variable lang. Dynamic client-based routines are embedded as JavaScript calls for vb_*.js files.
progressbar.js	Display of an animated progress bar (during software detection).
vb_Embed.js	Software status report routine. Prints information on missing software or displays a start button to enter the 3D world depending on the software status.
vb_RPDetect.js	RealPlayer detection routine.
vb_VRMLDetect.js	VRML plug-in detection routine.
vb_WebDetect.js	Web browser detection routine.
vb_vars.js	Setting of base URL, web root folder, and initial VRML file for main frame.
vb_Lang.js.php	Fetch localized translations from database and provide them as JavaScript variables. (Included by index0.php)

Table 4.1: Overview of files and corresponding tasks in /html folder

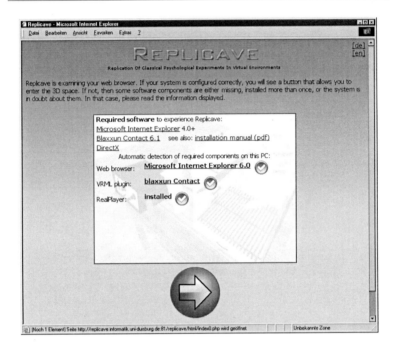

Figure 4.4: Replicave 2D start screen (after successful software detection)

4.4.2 Localization

On opening the file ./html/index0.php, the default language variable is stored in the PHP session variable[6] lang. The string type variable lang is set according to the language codes defined by the ISO 639-1 standard. The system supports English (en) as its default language and German (de).

The language variable is used to include language specific context-related translation tables at runtime. Due to the system's hierarchical file structure, translation tables are stored in a decentralized manner together with their corresponding 3D models. Localized texts for the framework system are defined in reserved files that are stored in language-specific subfolders of ./loc/ (translations.inc.php and instructions_lang.inc.php). The language-specific timeline image file is stored under the same location, as timeline_lang.png.

All language related routines read the session variable lang to determine the user-specified language. The language default and fallback variable $lang_standard

---

[6]While PHP variables are denoted with a leading "$", PHP session variables are not.

is stored in `./conf.inc.php` and is used if the session variable is undefined. Optionally, it can be used if any translation-related object is not found.

The PHP function tl(**$id**) that is defined in the file `./lib/trans.lib.php` implements an abstract translation function. The variable **$id** contains the variable name that is read from a language-specific translation table. Alternatively, the tl function can easily be adapted to read language-related data from other data sources.

4.4.3   File caching

In the default language version, the initial 3D world includes 7.26MB of data (242 files) that has to be transferred to the client. The actual data amount depends on the size of the localized information (text strings, multimedia files) and optionally transferred textures (for example, textures applied in LOD nodes in the gallery). Since both Microsoft Internet Explorer and BS Contact support client sided file caching, a cache size of at least 10MB is recommended for each application.

Cache	Size/Amount of files/Description
Internet Explorer	6.68MB/225/Total
	of which
	5.63MB/196/Image textures
	238KB/5/VRML data (dynamically generated)
	414KB/9/VRML data (static, compressed)
	398KB/15/Other files (HTML, ECMAScript,...)
BS Contact	6.27MB/212/Total
	of which
	3.52MB/98/Image textures (media room)
	2.34MB/105/Image textures (other)
	414KB/9/VRML data (static, compressed)

Table 4.2: Amount of cached data after transmission of the initial framework system

Static 3D-related files (VRML and image files) are stored in the BS Contact cache. All other files (including dynamically generated VRML files and static files referenced by dynamically generated files) are stored in the Internet Explorer cache (see Table 4.2). While the design of the data storage mechanism is partly redundant, the file transmission is not. Hence, 5.69MB of a total of 12.95MB of cached data is redundant but does not affect the data transmission time.

4.5   The 3D framework system

Replicave uses a building metaphor. In general, medium-bright and low-saturated colors have been used for objects that lack any primary functionality, while information-related objects have been designed in saturated colors to draw the user's attention.

The initial world visualizes the ground floor of a building that consists of the main hall, the gallery, the main media room, the vertical connector, and the horizontal connectors on higher levels, all of which are described in this section.

4.5.1   Main hall

The main hall has a cylindrical shape with a transparent half-sphere-shaped roof on top. The design is intended to reproduce the atmosphere of a modern museum building located in an urban environment which is visualized by a blue sky texture and externally placed building fragments that suggest an urban context (see Figure 4.5). The initial 3D file of the building's ground floor is ./framework/mainhall.wrl.php which contains inclusions of all other attached objects. The main hall's static 3D model is stored in ./framework/mainhall.wrl.

The exit door and the thresholds leading toward the main media room, the gallery, and the vertical connector are exclusively and equidistantly connected to the main hall, virtually dividing it into four quarter pie sections. The reception desk with a receptionist's avatar and the login terminal is located in the section between the gallery and the vertical connector. In addition, a dynamically generated information panel lists all contained experiments (./framework/contentlist.wrl.php). The experiment-related content is listed on an information plate located in front of the reception desk and on an interactive panel located within the elevator (see Section 4.5.4). Both content lists are generated dynamically at runtime according to the lab configuration settings (see Section 4.6.3).

The three other sections are decorated with items that underline the psychological context (images of psychologists[7]) and furniture objects.

The exit door is an interactive plane that allows the user to leave the system. It can be configured to initialize post-visit routines, such as opening a new browser window for an evaluation.

4.5.2   Gallery

The mainstream of psychology is presented in the gallery that was designed in an octagonal shape (see Figure 4.6). The design allows the installation of seven information-related walls and an eighth wall that provides space for the threshold

---

[7]In this thesis, the term 'psychologist' refers to researchers in the scientific domain of psychology.

to the main hall. The static 3D model (`./framework/gallery.wrl`) defines the outer walls and the transparent roof which follows the design of the main hall.

Large colored information boards display the various psychological research fields following the content and color design of a 2D-based timeline which was also designed in the context of the project [BLM+03b]. The information-related 3D objects are created by the dynamic script `./framework/gallery.wrl.php`. In front of each information board, individual information plates display a short curriculum vitae and a photograph of the psychologists mentioned on the board. Each plate has an interactive event sensor and an individual viewpoint configuration that allows the user to navigate there by simply clicking on them (jump navigation).

All text strings are defined as *string* parameters in `Text` nodes that use the proprietary *style* parameter "USE_TEXTURE" by which the BS VRML-plugin renders characters of true type fonts as image textures instead of geometrical models. Due to the large amount of text strings displayed in the gallery, the tablets are designed with `LOD` nodes[8] which reduces the amount of textures generated by the `Text` nodes. An alternative implementation based solely on the common VRML `Text` node proved that the usage of both techniques improved the rendering performance significantly.

As mentioned in Section 4.4.2, the text-based content is defined in translation tables that are stored in the `./loc/` folder. The psychologists' photographs are stored under `./framework/textures/infoterm/`. It is important to note that the gallery's text and image content is stored separately from the multimedia content of the laboratories and the media rooms.

4.5.3 Media rooms

The main media room on the ground floor offers multimedia documents about featured psychologists, regardless of any historical lab implementation. Since 3D lab design and implementation has to be considered as cost-intensive, Replicave uses a two-level approach. First, administrators or curators create a dedicated folder for a given psychologist under which multimedia documents are stored in a reserved `multimedia` subfolder. Then, the corresponding virtual labs are stored in other subfolders. The complete procedure is explained in Section 4.6.3.

As a result of this approach, the main media room provides access to the multimedia assets of all psychologists while the dedicated media rooms, that are accessible via the vertical connector (see Section 4.5.4), are solely created for psychologists who are featured with at least one historical laboratory.

The media room root files are `./framework/mroom_l.wrl.php`, for the (large) main media room on the ground floor, and `./framework/mroom_s.wrl.php`, for

---

[8]LOD (Level of detail) nodes provide distance information that are used by the browser to display appropriate versions of an object based on the distance from the user.

Figure 4.5: The main hall

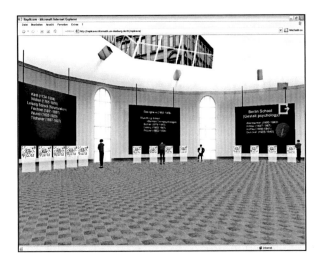

Figure 4.6: The gallery

the (small) dedicated media rooms, respectively.

Despite a different spatial layout and the limited amount of book shelves in the dedicated media room, where only one shelf is generated, they share the same functional elements and metaphors.

- For each psychologist, a **book shelf** PROTO is instantiated, the corresponding multimedia documents are parsed, and the shelf is filled with interactive 3D icons that represent either one of the multimedia document types book, movie, or picture.

- Each text document file is visualized by a **book** PROTO. In order to achieve a high degree of visual realism, each book's width, height, and cover textures are set randomly at runtime. The random textures are chosen from a set of three different book textures. Since the BS VRML-plugin lacks visualization support for text documents, each text document is hyperlinked by an Anchor node and opened in a new web browser window to prevent media discontinuity in the 3D frame. While the PROTO's url parameter defines the hyperlink target, the description parameter is used to visualize the document file name as a tool tip.

- Each image file is visualized in reduced size using a **picture frame** PROTO. Each picture frame has a constant default width and is scaled only along its y-axis according to the aspect ratio defined by the image size. Like the book PROTO, each picture-related ImageTexture node is embedded into an Anchor node that is hyperlinked to the corresponding image file. To prevent media discontinuity, all images are opened in a new web browser window.

- **Film rolls** depict RealPlayer movie files. Each roll is grouped with an individual TouchSensor node that is routed to the MovieTexture's url parameter of the silver screen. Hence, interactive movie selection is achieved by a mouse click. On a mouse over event, the movie file name is displayed as a tool tip.

- The **movie media controls** are integrated at the right side of the **film projector**. Here, play and stop buttons, iconified by a green triangle and a red square, can be used to start or stop the display of a movie selected by clicking on an interactive film roll icon. Each media control button uses an individual TouchSensor node. Due to the lack of a standardized media control API for movie data in VRML, the media control logic is implemented as a combination of Script nodes and routes. It is limited to a play and stop command.

- A **silver screen** serves as the central surface on which a selected movie is displayed. **Seating rows** are placed in front of the screen to draw the user's attention to the location of the screen and to highlight the functionality.

Multimedia type	File extension(s)
Text	pdf (Portable Document Format)
	html, htm (Hypertext Markup Language)
	txt (ASCII/plain text)
	doc (Microsoft Word Document)
	rtf (Rich Text Format)
Image	jpg, jpeg (JPEG)
	png (Portable Networks Graphics)
	gif (Graphics Interchange Format)
Movie	rm, ram (RealMedia Movie)

Table 4.3: Supported multimedia file extensions

- Various other **library furniture** objects such as sofas, armchairs, tables, plants, and lamps underline the ambiance of a library.

The mapping of multimedia file names to any of the multimedia document types text, image, or movie data is defined in the parseDir() function within the file ./framework/auxfunctions.inc.php. A list of all supported file extensions is given in Table 4.3. The routine is case-insensitive. Any unmatched file is filtered and not visualized.

The 3D icons are aligned in the following order: movies, text files, image files. The alignment sequence within each book shelf is from left-to-right, top-to-bottom.

In the main media room, the position of the book shelf depends on the overall amount of book shelves that are to be visualized. The alignment follows three simple directives, derived from the heuristics of user interface design and 3D interface design, respectively, by Dix [DFAB04, p.282] and Shneiderman [SP05, p.245]:

1. Each shelf is to be placed directly in front of the outer wall.

2. The shelves are to be sequentially aligned following a logical order.

3. The shelves should be recognized as an independent functional group.

The shelf creation is started from a dedicated corner of the room. Unlike the other corners in the main media room, the "shelf area" is designed basically as a bulge of dynamic size that, for large amounts of shelves, extends as a corridor of fixed width in a 45° angle from the adjacent static walls. The parallel walls for the corridor are not created unless space for more than five shelves is required. This architectural design pattern leads to a library area with convex outer walls[9]

---

[9]The convex hull property is restricted to the library area only.

so that the shelf objects are occlusion-free for any user located in front of them (see Figure 4.7).

The shelves are aligned clockwise and sequentially in alphabetical order. The corresponding psychologist's last name is printed in a non-serif capitalized font type above each shelf (see Figure 4.8).

4.5.4   Temporal metaphor

In analogy with the building metaphor, the temporal metaphor is an elevator, also referred to as the vertical connector. On each level, the elevator doors form a meta-threshold and give access to meta-paths. The desired path and destination threshold is defined by the user's selection of a different historical present on the elevator navigation panel. The panel is rendered dynamically at runtime and lists all available historical presents in chronological order with each psychologist's name and the title and year of his key experiment. A historical present is selected by a single mouse click one of the panel's entries. The dynamic interactive elevator navigation panel adapts automatically to changes in the content base depending on the available amount[10] of historical presents. All other elevator components are implemented in static VRML code. The file `./framework/vconnector.php` holds the dynamic part of the code and integrates the static code with an Inline node.

To minimize the amount of space required for paths and to allow the user to change quickly between two historical presents, the elevator is implemented with a passive path navigation. Once the user initiates a change request, the avatar's viewpoint is set to a position within the interior of the elevator and the elevator doors are closed. Otherwise, a user might interact with the navigation panel from a location outside of the elevator and be translocated without entering the elevator which would result in a logical inconsistency. This functionality also allows frequent users to use it as a shortcut navigation as demanded by common interface design heuristics [DFAB04, p.282ff.].

Since VRML viewpoint changes are only applicable for viewpoint nodes that are neither defined within PROTO nodes nor integrated by Inline nodes, the VRML code of the vertical connector file must be included directly in the VRML scene graph of the module requiring its functionality. This is achieved by using the PHP include command in the two modules that are connected by the vertical connector: `./framework/mainhall.wrl.php` and `./framework/hconnector.php`.

In order to minimize the cache access time when switching between the ground floor and visualizations of other building levels, automatic HTML frame resizing at runtime has been implemented. 3D worlds that are not part of the ground

---

[10]Originally planned for up to 6 historical presents, the panel's readability is still limited by the height and width of the elevator's back wall. If a future selection should exceed the amount of twelve panel entries, the design may have to be altered, for example, by reducing font sizes.

Figure 4.7: Dynamic alignment of media shelves in the main media room

Figure 4.8: Small media room with film projector and shelf

Listing 4.1: Frame switching (loader.php)

```
if(window.defaultStatus==" ") {
  parent.main.location.href="<?php print $link; ?>";
  setTimeout("load('main')",10000);
}
else {
  parent.histpresent.location.href=\
                          "<?php print $link; ?>";
  setTimeout("load('histpresent')",10000);
}
function load(whichFrame) {
  var Frame1=parent.document.getElementById("MainFrame");
  if(whichFrame=="histpresent") {
    Frame1.rows="*,100%";
    window.defaultStatus=" ";
  }
  else {
    Frame1.rows="100%,*"; window.defaultStatus="";
  }
}
```

Listing 4.2: Parameter initialization for historical present

```
if ($hc_root == 'now') {
  $_SESSION["hc_root"]       = $hc_root;
  $_SESSION["hc_position"] = -1;
  $_SESSION["vc_position"] = 0;
  $link = "mainhall.wrl.php";
} else {
  $_SESSION["hc_root"]       = $hc_root;
  $_SESSION["hc_position"] = -1;
  $_SESSION["vc_position"] = 1;
  $link = "hconnector.php";
}
```

floor are loaded in another HTML frame. Since VRML lacks support for an
event handler that returns information on the VRML file transmission progress,
the frame sizes of the main and the histpresent frame (see Figure 4.3) are switched
after a fixed time span of 10 seconds (see Listing 4.1). The routine is implemented
in the PHP script ./framework/loader.php. Each interactive element on the
elevator's navigation panel is hyperlinked with this loader routine and combined
with the target parameter $hc_root that is passed as a PHP "get" variable.

If a new historical present is selected by the user, the routine is loaded into the
loader HTML frame and performs three basic tasks: Depending on the $hc_root
string type variable (see Appendix A.2), a new target URL is defined as either
the ground floor's or the horizontal metaphor's root file. Then, the new target URL is loaded in an HTML frame. If $hc_root contains the reserved string
"now", the new target URL is set to the file containing the main access hall
(./framework/mainhall.wrl.php) and loaded in the main frame. Otherwise,
$hc_root is transformed into a PHP session variable and the new target URL is
set to the initial file containing the conceptional metaphor (./framework/hcon-
nector.php) and loaded in the histpresent frame. Finally, the frame displaying
the selected target URL is set to a height of 100% while the other is hidden and
the PHP session variables hc_root, hc_position, and vc_position are updated (see
Listing 4.2).

To maintain continuity, the user's avatar is initially located in the interior of
an identical copy of the elevator by setting his avatar to a new viewpoint that
visually corresponds with the former viewpoint. The human conception of an
elevator suggests that by using an elevator and looking at a different environment
as the doors reopen, one has changed places within a global coordinate system,
that is, one has passively moved along a given path. In fact, the user's avatar is
recreated in another 3D world. The existence of two dedicated frames, one for the
ground floor and a second for all other 3D worlds, has performance reasons. The

time required to recreate the ground floor is minimized by keeping an instance of the VRML viewer displaying it within a hidden frame in the background.

4.5.5 Template-based conceptional metaphor

In accordance with the system-wide concept of the building metaphor, the conceptional metaphor is modeled as a building floor. With regard to its implemented layout, the conceptional metaphor is also referred to as the horizontal connector. Due to performance reasons, neither the content of the connected laboratories nor the small media room are visualized. Instead, the content of each room is stored as a separate file and is loaded on demand, if the user navigates there by clicking on an interactive animated door.

The horizontal connector is based on parameterizable 3D model templates. Two templates are available: the building floor (`default` template) and a small-scaled simplified model of the building floor that serves as an interactive 3D map (`floor_ce` template). The template files are stored in subfolders of the `./framework/templates/` folder.

The main script file `./framework/hconnector.php` (see Listing 4.3) initially reads the PHP variables hc_root, hc_position (see Appendix A.2), lang, and template. Thereafter, standard string formatting and translation functions are defined. Finally, six mandatory template-specific functions are read and defined from a template configuration file named `template.inc.php` that must exist in each template's root subfolder that is set by the template variable. The functions are executed in the following order:

1. fetch_data($fn). Reads meta-data (for example, text descriptions) from a file or folder and defines global variables $data and $psyname.

2. create_viewpoint($hc_position). Define initial VRML viewpoint node according to the user's position.

3. create_domain($hc_root, $data, $lang). Generate VRML code for domain definintion.

4. create_places($hc_root, $data, $lang). Generate VRML code for place definintion.

5. create_paths($hc_root, $data, $lang). Generate VRML code for path definintion.

6. create_thresholds($hc_root, $data, $lang). Generate VRML code for threshold definintion.

Both templates refer to the hc_root variable that contains the unique folder name of the server sided web directory in the `./labs` folder in which the meta-data on the selected historical present is stored (see Section 4.5.4).

Listing 4.3: Template-based conceptional metaphor (hconnector.php)

```php
<?php
$hc_root      = $_SESSION["hc_root"];

$hc_position = $_SESSION["hc_position"];

if ($hc_position<0 OR $hc_position>6) {
  $hc_position=-1;
}

$lang         = $_SESSION["lang"];

$template     = $_GET["template"];

if (empty($template)) {$template="default";}

include("../lib/trans.lib.php");

include("../lib/alphanum.lib.php");

include("templates/$template/template.inc.php");

fetch_data('../labs/'.$hc_root.'/',$lang);

create_viewpoint($hc_position);
create_domain($hc_root, $data, $lang);
create_places($hc_root, $data, $lang);
create_paths($hc_root, $data, $lang);
create_thresholds($hc_root, $data, $lang);
?>
```

4.5.5.1   The `default` template

The building floor defined by the `default` template is implemented as a parameterizable 3D model. Its shape depends on the total amount of doors that are to be visualized. For a minimal visualization, the center of the floor, the door leading to the small media room, and one laboratory door are displayed. For a complete (maximal) layout, two side wings are added, each of which giving access to two laboratory doors while three doors (a single media room door, two laboratory doors) are visualized opposite the elevator (see Figure 4.9). The amount of six laboratory doors per floor suffices the project requirements with regard to the experiments that were originally intended for implementation.

The template's initialization file uses predefined auxiliary functions from the file `./framework/auxfunctions.inc.php` that are listed in Appendix A.3.

The `hc_position` variable has a default value of -1 which describes the avatar's viewpoint at the time of arrival in the elevator. Is is reset to -1 if the user changes the historical present by using the elevator and set to integer values between 0 and 6 if the user enters a door threshold to maintain the spatial integrity. New viewpoint positions are defined by appending an individual `hc_position` parameter definition to each door threshold's URL according to Table 4.4. If a user enters a room, the `hc_position` parameter is updated. Whenever the user leaves a laboratory room, the small media room, or the elevator, the `create_viewpoint` function automatically defines a viewpoint that is located inside of the floor near the threshold but oriented toward the center of the floor.

Due to the dynamic layout of the horizontal connector, the position and function of a door threshold is not identical for all possible amounts of lab rooms. For example, in a floor layout that features only one lab room, the small media room's threshold is located at position N3 while in layouts with more than one lab room it is at position N2. The threshold positions are assigned in the function `create_thresholds` (see Appendix A.5). The actual amount of laboratory doors to be created is defined by the length of the array `$labs_allowed` that is set in the historical present configuration file `psy.conf.inc.php` (see Section 4.6.3).

The connector's VRML code consists of static and dynamic 3D objects that are combined into a single VRML scene graph. For the dynamic placement of thresholds, seven positions (N1-N3, E1, E2, W1, W2) are reserved[11] on which the laboratory doors (L#1-L#6), the small media room door (SMR), or walls are allocated according to the layout matrix given in Table 4.4. The dynamic generation of the wings is achieved by including static VRML code fragments that either define a wall which renders a closure of the wing's entrance or the full wing layout. Code inclusion is controlled by a switch that displays a full east wing corridor for any amount of laboratories greater than two and the full west wing for

---

[11]The position definitions follow a geographical taxonomy that assumes that, within the given VRML coordinate system, the positive x-axis points southward and the positive y-axis eastward.

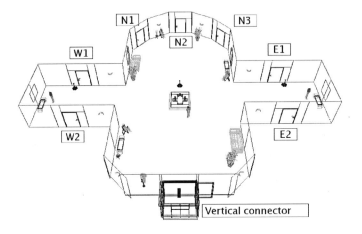

Figure 4.9: Conceptional metaphor with maximal amount of laboratories (wire-frame view with position descriptors)

any amount of laboratories greater than four. For smaller values, a wing opening is closed by a solid wall. The switchable static 3D object VRML files have the prefix hc_static_ and also include the definition of additional 3D objects, such as banks, avatars, and candelabra (see Figure 4.9). Due to the lack of support for an unlimited amount of light sources in DirectX, there are at most three PointLight nodes that coincide with the positions of the candelabrum objects.

For each threshold, the loader script ./framework/loader_room.php is called together with the target URL (variable url) and the door's hc_position parameter. The script is similiar to the aforementioned parameter initialization (see Listing 4.2) and is required for updating the session variable hc_position that allows a consistent viewpoint setting when re-entering the floor.

Target URLs include the small media room (./framework/mroom_s.wrl.php) and the laboratory doors' target URLs that are dynamically set as a concatenation of the ./labs/ prefix, its corresponding subfolder name as defined in $labs_allowed, and an /index.php suffix. A text description on each door indicates the name of the psychologist, the title of the experiment and its year of origin. The doors are aligned according to the element sequence defined in the array $labs_allowed. For easier user navigation, a room's content is indicated by the color of its outer door frame: small media room (blue), key experiment (green), or other preceding/succeeding experiments (white).

In addition, up to four images are automatically retrieved from the psychologist's multimedia assets that decorate the walls. Finally, a visual content explorer

#labs	position (with hc_position, if applicable)								
	N1 (1)	N2 (0)	N3 (2)	E1 (3)	E2 (4)	W1 (5)	W2 (6)	East wing	West wing
1	L#1	Wall	SMR	-	-	-	-	Wall	Wall
2	L#1	SMR	L#2	-	-	-	-	Wall	Wall
3	L#1	SMR	L#2	L#3	Wall	-	-	Wing	Wall
4	L#1	SMR	L#2	L#3	L#4	-	-	Wing	Wall
5	L#1	SMR	L#2	L#3	L#4	L#5	Wall	Wing	Wing
6	L#1	SMR	L#2	L#3	L#4	L#5	L#6	Wing	Wing

Table 4.4: Conceptional metaphor (layout matrix)

module, defined by the `floor_ce` template, is visualized in the center area of the floor.

4.5.5.2 The `floor_ce` template

The `floor_ce` template is a small-scaled simplified model of the `default` template described above. It is always generated within the `default` template and serves as an interactive 3D orientation map for content exploration. The floor is visualized in an abstract way: image textures and the elevator are not displayed. Each door object is replaced by a closed wall with an interactive cone that indicates a room. The cones are colored according to the color mapping used for the door frames in the `default` template. In addition, a room's content is displayed as a free-floating text above the map if the mouse pointer is moved over a cone. Based on the `default` template, the `floor_ce` template is likewise parameterizable.

4.5.6 Avatar design

Replicave's application domain focuses on providing users with an individualized 3D interactive space and client-based simulation-driven laboratories. In this section, the design and implementation of avatars with regard to design considerations for social and multi-user environments is discussed.

Available VRML-based collaborative virtual environments (CVEs), including Geometrek DeepMatrix[12] or Blaxxun Communication Server[13], offer only limited synchronization capabilities (avatar positions and rotations, streaming media) and, optionally, messaging functionality. Both products lack event synchronization of a Java-based simulation logic which would increase the cost of developing multi-user capable simulations because each simulation and all of its Java-EAI-based

---

[12]http://www.geometrek.com/
[13]http://www.blaxxuntechnologies.com/

PROTO name	Description
VisitorCouch	Male visitor in a casual sitting position.
VisitorStand	Male visitor in an upright standing position with arms crossed.
VisitorMovie	Male visitor in a sitting position watching straight ahead.
GuardChairRead	Museum guard sitting on a chair holding a paper sheet in his right hand and reading it.
GuardChairLook	Museum guard sitting on a chair. (Chair object is included.)
GuardInfoSheets	Museum guard bend over a dummy info sheet holder. (Sheet holder object is included.)
GuardTable	Museum guard in a standing position slightly leaning forward. (This avatar is well-suited for placement behind service counters.)

Table 4.5: Avatar PROTOs with description

clients would require experiment-specific synchronization functionalities. Furthermore, the majority of the interactive experiments is primarily intended for single participants.

Since basic personalized functionalities provided by the framework system imply the definition of individual 3D object properties at initialization time (for example, localized text strings, multimedia objects) as well as at runtime (for example, silver screen movie texture and animated film rolls during video data display) it is not feasible to implement both individual object-related features and a unique well-defined synchronizable 3D world model that is suitable for a 3D multi-user scenario.

A potential issue of single-user VEs is a low degree of telepresence experienced by its users due to the low degree of perceived agency. In a recent article, Nowak and Biocca discuss how system designers can respond to increase or maintain telepresence in VEs, showing that people respond socially to both human and computer-controlled entities, and that the existence of a virtual image increases telepresence [NB03]. Transferring these results on a single-user VE in the museum domain, agents with a human-like behavior and visual appearance should increase the telepresence.

Three steps lead to an agent design:

1. Definition of primary groups of persons in a museum or an exhibition from

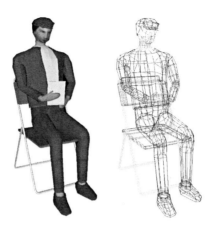

Figure 4.10: Textured and wireframe visualization of PROTO GuardChairRead

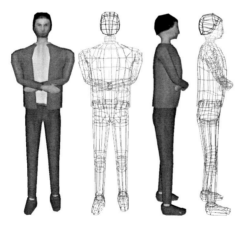

Figure 4.11: Textured and wireframe visualization of PROTO VisitorStand (front and side view)

a visitor's perspective.

2. Definition of the groups' primary behavior patterns.

3. Definition of typical visual appearances of individual group members.

Two primary groups of persons can be identified from a visitor's perspective: visitors and museum staff working in the exhibition area, that is, museum guards. In classic exhibition environments, standard behavior patterns of visitors include standing, sitting, walking, and watching exhibition or interacting with additional media (reading info board, watching movies). Behavior pattern of guards in exhibitions include sitting or standing still near exhibition objects or along paths. As a visit to a common arts or science museum approves, visitors will most likely be dressed in casual or business clothes, while museum guards will most likely wear some sort of uniform.

According to these considerations, three visitor and four museum guard avatars were designed with the Blender modeling tool in a study project during the winter term 2005/06. A data format export script was developed that generates VRML code from Blender's internal data format.

The avatars were designed and modeled but not animated. The export filter was not completely H-Anim 200x-compliant with regard to animation behavior which resulted in irregularities during body part animation. Assuming that fully H-Anim 200x-compliant avatars could have been generated, they would still lack an "intelligent" control logic and body motion data. Hence, animation support for the avatars was regarded as too cost-extensive.

The standard behavior patterns mentioned above were applied to static avatars by focusing on behaviors that do not imply any animation, motion, or interaction and by defining still body postures that imply a preoccupation or an unavailability for communication requests in order to minimize the user's expectation for a potential interaction or to serve as a feature demonstration. For example, the movie display feature in the large media room is indicated by an instance of the VisitorMovie avatar sitting in an armchair in front of the movie projection screen. Additional motionless behavior patterns were defined for visitors (standing or sitting in front of an exhibition or information object and watching the same) and for museum guards (sitting or standing motionless along the paths or near thresholds).

Standing visitors are visualized in a closed body posture with arms crossed. Guard postures include reading, watching, and sorting sheets. Only the guard model for the reception desk was designed in an open posture to underline the interactivity of the nearby login terminal.

Seven avatar models were designed and exported to individual VRML PROTOs that are stored in the avatar library ./framework/ProtoAvatars.wrl. An overview and two exemplary visualizations are given in Table 4.5 and Figures 4.10

and 4.11, respectively. The avatar's face image texture is based on the computer-generated face entitled "m(1-32)" described in the article "Beautycheck" by Braun *et al.* [BGMS01, p.72].

4.5.7 Heads-Up display

The PROTO library ./framework/GUIObjects3D.wrl includes various standardized objects for a Heads-Up display (HUD) including interactive, animated 3D buttons for information (Icon_Info), an exit shortcut (Icon_Exit), and a customizable icon for individual textures (Icon_TexturedPanel). The information visualization is provided by a semi-transparent message box for text (Messagebox) and images (GraphicalMessagebox) which are based on the proprietary Layer3D node.

There are four predefined context-specific HUD layouts, as described in Table 4.6. For reasons of consistency, each layout generates three visually identical 3D buttons at fixed screen locations with identical but context-specific functionalities (see Figures 4.5, 4.6, and 4.7).

HUD filename	Description
GUI_framework.inc.wrl.php	Ground floor layout.
GUI_hconnector.inc.wrl.php	Conceptional metaphor layout.
GUI_mroom_s.inc.wrl.php	Small media room layout.
GUI_lab.inc.wrl.php	Lab room layout (optional).

Table 4.6: Predefined HUD layouts with description

The timeline button gives access to a large 2D timeline image that visualizes the mainstream of psychology over the last two centuries. The exit button allows the user to move from one spatial and temporal location to one that is hierarchically higher: from a lab room to the conceptual metaphor, from the conceptual metaphor to the ground floor, and from the ground floor to an URL outside the 3D environment.

The information button provides the user with text-based context-specific instructions. Except of the lab room layout, the text instructions are defined in a localized instruction text file (see Section 4.4.2). By default, the lab room HUD layout reads instructions from a localized experiment-specific file, called loc_*lang*.inc.php, that is stored in an experiment's dedicated folder (see Section 4.6.2). The lab room HUD layout is optional. It can be replaced or completed by other interactive objects with regard to an experiment's requirements.

With regard to its assigned spatial domain, a HUD layout script is called from within the PHP script that generates that VRML-based domain by utilizing a PHP include() function. The HUD should be generated in the scenegraph's root level and must be generated after the default viewpoint [BC97a, p.336].

Listing 4.4: Text3D PROTO (Header)

```
PROTO Text3D [
   exposedField SFBool    IsInput     FALSE
   exposedField SFBool    IsSecret    FALSE
   exposedField MFString  StaticText  ""
   exposedField SFVec3f   translation 0 0 0
   exposedField SFVec3f   scale 0.5 0.5 0.5
   exposedField MFString  TextureURL  "font.png"
   exposedField SFColor   TextColor 0.8 1 0.75
   exposedField SFBool    DSActive    FALSE
   exposedField SFString  Input       ""
   exposedField SFBool    IsComplete  FALSE
   exposedField SFInt32   state 0
   exposedField SFBool    IsPressEnter  FALSE
   exposedField SFBool    SpaceAllowed  FALSE
   exposedField SFInt32   minlength 1
   exposedField SFInt32   maxlength 12
   field MFString  family  "Courier New"
   field SFString  style   "BOLD USE_TEXTURE"
   field SFFloat   size    0.95]
   {...}
```

4.5.8   Text3D PROTO

A PROTO called Text3D (see Listing 4.4) was developed that provides a parameterizable software interface for both text input and output within the 3D environment. Since native text input is not supported by VRML97, it utilizes Bitmanagement's proprietary DeviceSensor node to read alpha-numeric character input from a standard PC keyboard. The Text3D PROTO, stored in ./framework/Proto-Text3d.wrl, is multi-functional and can be used for the following functionalities:

- Non-interactive text display.

- Interactive confirmation (Wait until enter key is pressed).

- Interactive text input form field.

- Interactive password input form field.

In any mode, the text string contained in *StaticText* is printed first. Input modes are activated by setting *IsInput* or *IsPressEnter* to true, for password input *IsSecret* must also be set to true. A blinking cursor indicates the interactive mode. The minimum and maximum length of the input string is determined by *minlength* and *maxlength*, respectively. *SpaceAllowed* determines whether or not the space key is read. Entered characters are visualized and stored in a concatenated form as a (clear text) string value, called *Input*, that stores the input string. The font used for the visualization is set in the field *family*. The *style* field value "USE_TEXTURE" requires a proprietary Text node extension provided by the VRML plugin. It results in an automatically rendered bitmapped font texture based on the (geometrically defined true type) font set in the field *family*. As a result, text is rendered much faster. However, the font must be installed on the client PC. For the usage of special fonts or to ensure the usage identical fonts on all clients, the PROTO can be manually adapted and configured for usage with a predefined font texture image file in the PNG file format (*TextureURL*). The text color is defined by *TextColor*.

For performance reasons, interactive Text3D PROTO instances should be controlled through a Script node in *DirectOutput* mode. Each instance of the Text3D PROTO provides its own DeviceSensor node that must be activated with an explicit value assignment. The input mode and the corresponding DeviceSensor's activity are terminated by pressing the key with the ASCII keycode 13, which usually corresponds to the keyboard's "enter" key. Furthermore, the field value *IsComplete* is set to true. Thereafter, the control script can process the input string.

This allows the implementation of standardized interaction sequences, such as a login procedure that utilizes a username and password form fields.

For performance reasons, a DeviceSensor should only be activated if needed and no more than one should be active at a time.

4.6 Data storage and management

As a web-based information system, Replicave serves as a publishing platform for various file formats and data types including text-based files (VRML, PHP, JavaScript, PHP, HTML) and binary files (compressed VRML files, multimedia files, Java applets). Due to the diversity of the involved data formats, the amount of files and the requirement for a hierarchically organized content management, a file-based document management system was installed.

In addition, some experiments require the storage of user-generated experimental data records which implies a central database for general user data and experiment-related data.

In this section, the relational database management system (RDBMS) and the document management system (DMS) are described. Finally, the content-related configuration files and directories are explained in detail.

4.6.1   The **VirtLab** Database

The VirtLab database is a MySQL database that can be administered via a
phpMyAdmin[14] web interface. It is exclusively used for two types of data:

1. User and learning group administrative data.

2. Data that is dynamically generated during the conduction of an experiment
   either by the user or by a simulation control logic.

The framework system provides a database access library that allows transparent
access to the database (./lib/dbconnect.inc.php). In single-session experiments, users can be identified by the unique PHP variable session ID. In experiments that require multiple sessions or group identification, a user authentication
is required. Due to the focus on an exhibition of historical laboratories, user authentication is optional. Users can authenticate themselves at the terminal in
the main hall by entering a username and a password. In addition, group-related
data can be entered. The user can assign himself to a user group, create a new
user group or proceed to use the system with a single user account. User logins
to the system are stored in the table *logins* (see Figure 4.12).

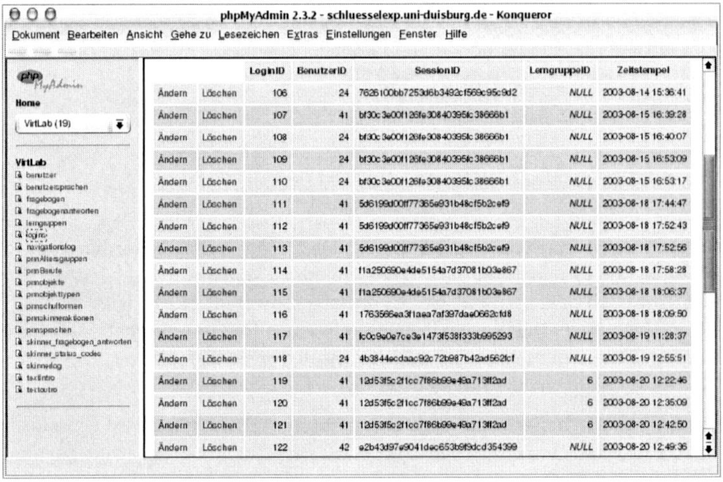

Figure 4.12: VirtLab database (phpMyAdmin displaying table *logins*)

---

[14]http://www.phpmyadmin.net/ [Accessed 20 June 2006]

Furthermore, the database can optionally be used to store user-generated or simulation-generated data for further analysis. In this case, the database administrator has to create one or more dedicated tables for data storage. Although the system provides a database, an evaluation, analysis, or visualization of user-generated or simulation-based data will require additional tools which are not included in the framework system.

The framework system's 3D model can be extended to monitor the user's navigation path through the system. This technique requires VRML sensor nodes on various locations, preferably thresholds, throughout the 3D world logging the sessionID, the triggered object (ObjektID), sensor type (TypID), and a time stamp, and, optionally, the username (LoginID).

In addition, the evaluation system PHP Surveyor[15] uses MySQL as its database backend. However, it uses the default database phpsurveyor for storing survey data.

4.6.2 The document management system

Replicave uses the open-source software Philex[16] for the file and folder administration. According to the classification by Rothfuss and Ried [RR01, pp. 59ff.], Philex is a DMS[17]. It features user administration, web-based file and folder management with basic operations (create, delete, copy, paste), editing of text-based files, configurable access restriction regardless of file content, and a user interface with tree-based folder visualization (see Figure 4.13).

In comparison to other file-oriented transfer and administration services, like SSH or FTP, the PHP-based Philex is accessed via the web browser using the HTTP protocol and uses the MySQL database for the storage of user-related data (login, password, root folder). Hence, there is no requirement for any additional server software or protocols.

Due to the hierarchical folder structure and multi-user support, content is grouped in dedicated folders and managed via the DMS. At least five administrator or curator roles can be deduced by setting user-specific root folders. A role overview with regard to role title, root folder, task description, and the primary task-related file or folder[18] is given in Table 4.7. For all roles, the access rights imply read and write access to the user-specific root folder and all of its subfolders, respectively.

---

[15]http://www.phpsurveyor.org/ [Accessed 17 June 2006]

[16]http://sourceforge.net/projects/philex/ [Accessed 11 October 2004]

[17]According to the definition by Rothfuss and Ried, Philex is not an asset management system, because it does not focus on special media or file types. However, by restricting user access to special subfolders only, it can be configured as such.

[18]File and folders mentioned are located relative to the corresponding root folder.

Replicave administrator (root folder: /replicave/)	
Framework administration	`framework`, `html`, `lib`, `loc` (folders)
Replicave content administrator (root folder: /replicave/labs/)	
Definition of psychologist-related folder name(s) containing content approved for publication.	`main.conf.inc.php`
Create/Remove folder(s) containing all experiments and multimedia files for a psychologist.	*psychologist* (folder)
Dedicated curator (root folder: /replicave/labs/*psychologist*/)	
Definition of folder name(s) containing experiments approved for publication.	`psy.conf.inc.php`
Administration of multimedia content	`multimedia` (folder)
Administration of localized meta-data	`loc_`*lang*`.inc.php` (files)
Create/Remove folder containing laboratory data	*lab* (folder)
Dedicated multimedia administrator (root folder: /replicave/labs/*psychologist*/multimedia/)	
Administration of multimedia content	`multimedia` (folder and localized sub-folders)
Lab curator (root folder: /replicave/labs/*psychologist*)	
Default lab initialization file	`index.php`

Table 4.7: Overview of roles, tasks, and related files or folders

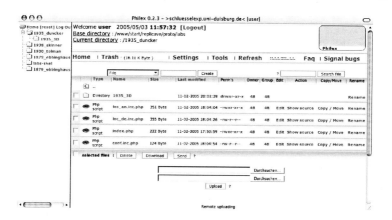

Figure 4.13: The Philex document management system

4.6.3 Content-related configuration files and directories

The ./labs folder contains all experiment-related data and the psychologist-related multimedia files. Its predefined folder structure a allows dynamic information visualization by PHP modules that analyze configuration files and generate a context-related layout. In this section, selected files and folders and their specific configuration options or structure are explained with regard to the laboratory-related content and the roles given in Table 4.7.

The main laboratory configuration file is named main.conf.inc.php and contains two arrays: psychos_allowed and psychos_mediaonly. The elements of both arrays define psychologist-specific folder names that must exist in the ./labs folder. The array psychos_mediaonly lists folder names of psychologists whose presentation is limited to multimedia content in the main media room. The array psychos_allowed lists psychologist's dedicated folders that, in addition to multimedia content, also contain at least one virtual laboratory (that is, one historical present) that is intended for publication. Both arrays must contain disjoint entries.

Each psychologist's dedicated folder must contain a configuration file, named psy.conf.inc.php, localized meta-data files, and a multimedia folder, named multimedia. The configuration file psy.conf.inc.php defines a single array labs_allowed that lists all subfolders that contain laboratories which are intended for publication. The activation of a psychologist's dedicated folder in the file main.conf.inc.php implies that at least one valid folder entry is defined in the labs_allowed array of the corresponding psy.conf.inc.php file. Any psychologist-related folder that is intended for publication must feature localized meta-data

Listing 4.5: Localized metadata file (Duncker experiment)

```php
<?php
$tl_name          =  "Duncker";
$tl_firstname     =  "Karl";
$tl_yearborn      =  "1903";
$tl_yeardeceased  =  "1940";
$tl_keyfolder     =  "1926_candle";
$tl_topic         =  "Functional fixedness";
?>
```

that is defined in files named loc_*lang*.inc.php, *lang* being the ISO-639-1 compliant language code (see Section 4.4.2). Six variables are defined in the localized metadata files: $tl_firstname, $tl_name (psychologist's first and last name, respectively), $tl_yearborn, $tl_yeardeceased (the year of birth and the year of death), $tl_keyfolder (the subfolder name that contains the historical key experiment), and $tl_topic (the scientific topic of the historical key experiment or the psychological theory). An exemplary file is given in Listing 4.5.

The reserved `multimedia` folder and its subfolders contain all psychologist-related multimedia assets for a visualization in the media rooms. Basically, all multimedia files stored in the `multimedia` folder are parsed and visualized. Language dependent content, such as movies, biographies, or images that contain written text can be stored in subfolders named according to the ISO-639-1 language code. Multimedia assets stored in a language-specific subfolder are only parsed and visualized if the folder name matches the selected language code. Furthermore, a folder named `original` contains multimedia source documents in data formats that are required for content creation but are not suited for publication. The latter folder is not parsed by any module but allows dedicated curators to easily modify existing content or to translate it into other languages.

Each laboratory is initially loaded by opening a file named `index.php`. The script-based initialization file offers a high degree of flexibility. Generally, each laboratory room must feature an exit that must be hyperlinked to the horizontal connector by reading the corresponding variable hc_root. Existing 3D worlds can be embedded by using the printfile auxiliary function (see Appendix A.3).

An overview of the mentioned files and directories is given in Appendix A.4.

Chapter 5

The replicated experiments

In this chapter, the psychological theories of Ebbinghaus, Skinner, Duncker, Tolman, and Sperling are introduced based, unless indicated otherwise, on the psychological course book "Wege in die Psychologie" by G. Mietzel [Mie98]. The conceptual design of each experiment is outlined, and the experiment-specific implementations based on the modeling pipeline (see Section 3.3) are described with a focus on 3D asset acquisition and the simulation/interaction model.

5.1 Skinner: Operant conditioning

B.F. Skinner's (1904-1990) theory is based upon the idea that learning is a function of change in overt behavior. Changes in behavior are the result of an individual's response to stimuli that occur in the environment. The occurrence of a stimulus or event following a response that increases the likelihood of that response being repeated is called reinforcement. Reinforcement is the key element in Skinner's stimulus-response theory. A positive reinforcer is anything that leads to an increased response frequency. Withdrawal of a positive reinforcer leads to a decrease in the amount of occurrence of the corresponding behavior ("extinction"). Negative reinforcement means that a response frequency increases when an adverse stimulus is withdrawn or is successfully avoided.

Skinner published various schedules of reinforcement (for example, fixed-interval, variable-interval, fixed-ratio, variable-ratio schedule) and their effects on establishing, maintaining, and extinguishing behavior. During his first experiments, Skinner used a straight tunnel through which the rats had to walk before receiving a stimulus at the other end. Due to the experiment's work-intensive reinitialization process, that is, relocating the animal from the end to the start of the tunnel, Skinner designed and built a circular tunnel mounted on a rotatable horizontal axis that provided an equal balance for an empty construction and allowed a slope to either side if a rat was wandering through it. Skinner also developed a cumulative recorder, the so-called kymograph, for automated recording of the response rate. An interactive food dispenser allowed automated reinforcement delivery. In the late 1930s, he constructed the so-called Skinner box, which typically contains one or more levers that an animal can press, one or more stimulus lights, and one or more places, in which reinforcers, such as food, can be delivered. Delivery of other reinforcers, such as water, or negative enforcers, like electric shock through the floor of the chamber, was also possible.

Primary sources were various books by B.F. Skinner [Ski38, Ski59, Ski84]. Secondary sources include the biography "B.F. Skinner - A life" by D.W. Bjork [Bjo93], extracts from educational films by FIM Psychologie at the University of Erlangen-Nuremberg [Ang79], and photographic material provided by the B.F. Skinner foundation[1], Morgantown, West Virginia. The sources were evaluated in co-operation with the department of psychology. Then, storyboards for the following scenarios were written:

- Rat in the tunnel

- Rat in the circular tunnel with kymograph

And, based on the 1938 Skinner box:

- Observing operant behavior of a rat

- Shaping a rat

- Observing reinforcement plans

- Observing discriminative stimuli

5.1.1   2D prerendered animation

The scenarios "Rat in the tunnel", "Observing operant behavior of a rat", and "Shaping a rat" were reconstructed as 2D interactive Flash animations by staff of the department of psychology. The scenario "Rat in the circular tunnel with kymograph" was depicted in static Flash-based slides. The results of the project's 2D-based track were published as additional online supplements to G. Mietzel's course book [Wor04]. However, the 2D implementations were not based on any complex non-deterministic behavior simulation model. Instead, prerendered animation sequences were replayed after user interaction.

---

[1]http://www.bfskinner.org/ [Accessed 17 May 2006]

5.1.2   Replication focus for a 3D-based reconstruction

Based on the scenario drafts "Observing reinforcement plans" and "Observing discriminative stimuli" 3D asset requirements and simulation/interaction models for the two modified scenarios

- Observing reinforcement plans and discriminative stimuli in a fixed-interval schedule of reinforcement and

- Observing reinforcement plans and discriminative stimuli in a fixed-ratio schedule of reinforcement

were developed that both represent key experiments. The 3D replication focuses on historical experiments in which the 1938 Skinner box was used. The preceding 2D-based experiments described in Section 5.1.1 were not ported to 3D.

Each of the two new scenarios has been structured in three phases. As in his historical experiments, Skinner used a self-designed mechanism situated outside of the box for controlling food delivery. During the first phase a food pellet is delivered every time the food lever is pressed. During the second phase, the mechanism is configured not to deliver a reward for every response. Skinner defined two reinforcement plans: fixed-ratio schedule and fixed-interval schedule. Fixed-ratio schedule means that a reward is given only after a fixed number n of responses $(n > 1)$. In fixed-interval schedule, reward delivery is suspended for a time interval of fixed length. During the third phase, punishment is demonstrated by applying electric shock for every response.

5.1.3   A time and state based simulation model

There are only few papers concerned with modeling or simulation of rat behavior. In parts I and II of their articles entitled "The dynamics of long-term exploration in the rat", O. Tchernichovski, Y. Benjamini, and I. Golani have described exploratory behavior patterns in rats [TBG98]. First, empirical data was gathered. Then, behavior patterns were scrutinized and a first approximation hypothesis was formulated as a descriptive model. In part II, an analytic model, based on a dynamical system, with few assumptions concerning motivation and learning, was proposed by which the empirical findings could be explained and approximated [TB98].

In a paper entitled "Open field behavior in a rat - a computer simulation", N. Buderham and H. Lifshitz have described open field behavior of rats by means of a computer simulation [BL00]. The Matlab model consists of two main components: an agent that incorporates the internal factors curiosity, security, and memory and an environment containing external representations of motivations. The implementation included a 2D path visualization.

A commercial stand-alone interactive software application called Sniffy allows to conduct Skinner's operant conditioning experiment. Its theoretical foundations are explained in the article "Sniffy, the virtual rat: Simulated operant conditioning" by J. Graham, T. Alloway, and L. Krames [AGK94]. The authors report on the use of the simulation tool to teach Skinner's experiment concerning operant conditioning to 900 undergraduate psychology students. The purpose of the Sniffy application is to visualize and communicate the methods of training, shaping, acquisition, and extinction of conditioned behavior. The program allows to demonstrate the principles of continuous and partial reinforcement and extinction. The animation sequences have been rendered from captured still pictures of a rat in a Skinner box. The rat has been filmed showing activities, such as wandering around, turning around, lever-pressing, and eating. Actions are controlled by a random function for modeling baseline behavior and a logistic function for modeling different states of operant behavior.

The first part of a Sniffy session deals with the observation of the rat's untrained behavior during which the learner is expected to denote the frequency of moving, rearing against walls, and lever presses. Thereafter, positive reinforcers can be used to motivate the rat to press the lever more frequently, which can be accomplished by dropping a pellet into the food bowl immediately after the rat presses the bar. Reinforcement can be paired with secondary stimuli like sound or light. A lamp situated over the bar and a sound signal can be interactively operated by the user.

Model development

With regard to the replication focus, a state-based model has been developed that is primarily based on inhomogeneous Markov chains over a finite state space and includes several concepts of the Sniffy tool.

Definition 5.1 Let $P^{(1)}, P^{(2)}, \ldots$ be a sequence of $(k \times k)$-matrices, each of which satisfies

$$P_{i,j} \geq 0 \text{ for all } i, j \in \{1, .., k\}$$

and

$$\Sigma_{j=1}^{k} P_{i,j} = 1 \text{ for all } i \in \{1, .., k\}$$

A random process $X = (X_t)_{t=0,1,2,\ldots}$ with finite state space $S = \{s_1, \ldots, s_k\}$ is called an **inhomogeneous Markov chain with transition matrices** $P^{(1)}, P^{(2)}, \ldots$, if for all n, all $i, j \in \{1, .., k\}$ and all $i_0, \ldots, i_{n-1} \in \{1, .., k\}$ we have

$$\mathbf{P}(X_{n+1} = s_j \mid X_n = s_i, X_{n-1} = s_{i_{n-1}}, ..., X_1 = s_{i_1}, X_0 = s_{i_0})$$
$$= \mathbf{P}(X_{n+1} = s_j \mid X_n = s_i)$$
$$= P_{i,j}^{(n+1)}.$$

Markov chains have the so-called Markov property (that is, they are memoryless) and are usually represented through

1. A transition matrix

$$(p_{ij}(t)) = P_{i,j} = \begin{pmatrix} p_{11}(t) & \cdots & p_{1k}(t) \\ \vdots & \ddots & \vdots \\ p_{k1}(t) & \cdots & p_{kk}(t) \end{pmatrix}$$

with transition probabilities

$$p_{ij}(t) := P(X_{t+1} = s_j \mid X_t = s_i), \, i, j = 1, ..., k$$

or

2. A directed weighted state graph $G = (S, E, w)$, with $(s_i, s_j) \in E$, for all $i, j \in \{1, ..., k\}$ and weight function $w(s_i, s_j) = p_{ij}(t)$ for all $(s_i, s_j) \in E$, called the transition graph.

Before defining states and detailed controls, a process flow of the model is defined. A rat is considered as an agent in a specific conditioning state that implies certain expectations based on previous memorized experiences. The active conditioning state (or expectation state) determines further possible actions and with corresponding transition probabilities. Each agent action causes a reaction from the environment, for example, "pressing the food lever" may cause the reaction "receive pellet" or "move" may cause "nothing".

Depending on the reaction and the active conditioning phase, existing experiences and implied expectations can be altered. A process-based representation of the rat model is depicted in Figure 5.1. The terminology is partly based on the theory of Markov decision processes (MDP), which are used for optimizing S-R-models with regard to "behavior strategies", that is, finding an action sequence through which a rewarding function is maximized [Put94]. Since we intend to design a reversible non-deterministic model that simulates a time-dependent learning process of a rat, including "non-optimized" behavior strategies, the MDP technique is not directly applicable. Based on the model given in Figure 5.1, various finite state sets can be defined.

The ground plane of the box has been divided into a $(2m + 1) \times (2m + 1)$ checkerboard, with $m = 1$. Hence, the plane is organized as a 3×3 checkerboard

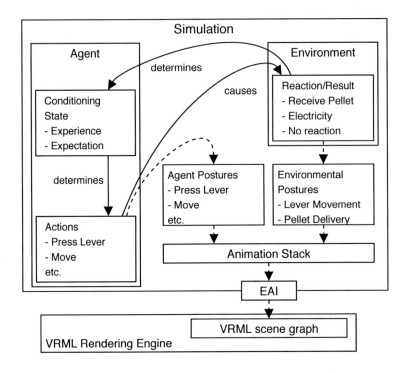

Figure 5.1: Simulation model (process flow)

indexed with field numbers 1..9. Interactive objects, such as the lever and food dispenser are situated on the wall and are accessible through field 2. Field adjacency is defined through a 4-neighborhood topology with neighboring fields in the north (N), west (W), east (E), and south (S) of the actual position. Let $S_\theta = F \times D$ be the **position state set** where $F = \{1, .., 9\}$ is the field set and $D = \{N, W, S, E\}$ the direction set.

Visual animations are composed of the postures moving up (*GetUp*) and down (*GetDown*), moving forward by one field (*MoveForward*), turn clockwise (*TurnRight*), turn counter-clockwise (*TurnLeft*), waiting (*Wait*), and lever pressing (*SetMark*). Postures correspond to implemented 3D animations for visualization. Let $S_\pi = \{$ *GetUp, GetDown, MoveForward, TurnRight, TurnLeft, Wait, SetMark* $\}$ be the **posture state set**.

As in the Sniffy model, the rat model should take actions based on expectations. Instead of a variable used in the Sniffy model, we define an **expectation state set** $S_\eta = \{$ *Unconditioned, AlwaysPellet, RatioPellet, IntervalPellet, Electricity, Experienced* $\}$, as described in Table 5.1.

State	Agent expectation	Initial probability (lever pressing)
Unconditioned (0)	No expectation of reward.	Low
AlwaysPellet (1)	Conditioned. Agent is expecting reward for action.	High
RatioPellet (2)	Conditioned. Agent "knows" that lever pressing is likely to deliver reward and continues action during fixed-ratio schedule.	Very high
IntervalPellet (2')	Conditioned. Agent "knows" that reward delivery depends on a time interval Δt.	Very high (at begin and end of Δt) Low (at other times)
Electricity (3)	Agent is aware of delivery of electrical current.	Very low
Experienced (4)	After extinction, the agent can be reconditioned faster than in state 0.	Low

Table 5.1: Expectation states for reward delivery (Skinner experiment)

During both scenarios, the active reinforcement plan determines the environ-

ment-specific reactions that are technically identical to various reward delivery phases. Let $S_\varphi = \{NO\_PELLETS,\ ALWAYS\_PELLETS,\ RATIO\_PELLETS,$
$GET\_ELECTRICITY,\ INTERVAL\_PELLETS\}$ be the environment-based **phase
state set.**

State transitions depend primarily on the environment's reaction $r \in R$, where
$R = \{GOT\_PELLET,\ GOT\_NOTHING,\ GOT\_ELECTRICITY\}$ is the reaction
set. Since we intend to design a simple model, the food lever is the only interactive
object resulting in no reaction or in delivery of either food or an electric current.

An estimation of the complexity of a model based entirely on the above-mentioned
state sets leads to $|S_\varphi \times S_\eta \times S_\pi \times S_\theta| = 5{\cdot}6{\cdot}7{\cdot}9{\cdot}4 = 7560$ states and would result
in a (7560×7560)-transition matrix with 57153600 elements for each reaction $r \in$
R, not including additional states for compensation of memory-specific issues,
which have not yet been considered.

Based on this estimation, three problems must be solved with regard to lower
complexity and feasibility of implementation:

- Which states $s \in S_\varphi \times S_\eta \times S_\pi \times S_\theta$ are required?

- Which transition probabilities with $p > 0$ are required?

- How are time-awareness and time-dependent actions modeled with regard
  to observable learning, developing expectations, and memory?

Based on the phase set S_φ and expectation set S_η, we define two pairs of phase
and expectation sequences:

- Phase sequence $(rp_k) = (ALWAYS\_PELLETS,\ RATIO\_PELLETS,\ GET\_-$
  $ELECTRICITY,\ ALWAYS\_PELLETS)$ and expectation sequence
  $(re_k) = (Unconditioned,\ AlwaysPellet,\ RatioPellet,\ Electricity,\ Experienced)$
  for the fixed-ratio scenario, and

- Phase sequence $(ip_k) = (ALWAYS\_PELLETS,\ INTERVAL\_PELLETS,$
  $GET\_ELECTRICITY,\ ALWAYS\_PELLETS)$ and expectation sequence
  $(ie_k) = (Unconditioned,\ AlwaysPellet,\ IntervalPellet,\ Electricity,\ Experi-$
  $enced)$ for the fixed-interval scenario.

A discrete time counter is used for compensation of the Markov property, especially during the fixed-interval scenario. Phase transitions depend on the occurrence of user interaction (manual phase transition) or model-based expectation
state transitions. In the latter case, a phase transition occurs after a time interval (countdown) that is started when the agent's expectation state matches the
reaction state of the environment, that is, when the agent has "learned" and has
adapted its behavior to the reaction of the environment (see Figure 5.2).

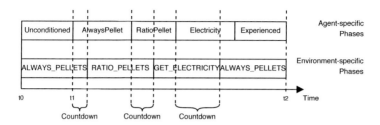

Figure 5.2: Phase and expectation sequences in fixed-ration scenario (time-dependent representation)

Within each expectation state s_{η_i}, the agent "behaves" according to actions that correspond to a single posture or are composed of a posture sequence. We define an action state set $S_\alpha = \{Field(1),...,Field(9), SITUP\_AND\_BEG, SetMark\}$ where the action $SITUP\_AND\_BEG$ is a posture sequence ($GetUp, GetDown$) and the actions $Field(i)_{i=1,...,9}$ are posture sequences dynamically generated at run-time that are composed of all required turning and movement postures for a movement from some field k to a destination field i. The action $SetMark$ is identical to the posture $SetMark$.

In each expectation state, the action states S_α form a random walk where $SetMark$ is the only action, which might lead to an expectation state transition. Therefore, the transition probabilities of the random walk primarily depend on the probability of the action $SetMark$, that is, lever pressing and the environment's reaction determined by the phase state.

In the model proposed by Alloway $et\ al.$ transition probabilities p_{st} are influenced by a logistic behavior frequency function $fr_z(x) = g + \frac{m-g}{1+exp(\frac{-x+d}{c})}$ where x is the reinforcement level in state z, g and m are frequency limits, d a threshold, and c a scale slope factor. In a state based model Markov chains must be adapted to model the agent's learning progress.

Our primary assumption is that the attraction of the reinforcement-specific action $SetMark$ is only modified after a reaction of the environment to this action. Otherwise, the transition probabilities of the random walk remain unmodified. Since location-specific probabilities can easily be defined or altered to control the "attraction" of a single field, we have focused on altering the probability of the action $SetMark$ only, assuming a proceeding adaption of the other random walk probabilities. For example, with each pellet received during the phase $ALWAYS\_PELLETS$, an increasing drift directed toward field 2 must be generated through increasing those transition probabilities leading to movements toward this location and to the action taken there.

In both scenarios, the state-based part of the model uses expectation states s_{η_i}

that are characterized by two properties:

- Each expectation state s_{η_i} has exactly one potential successor $s_{\eta_{i+1}}$, as defined by the expectation sequences (re_k) (see Figure 5.2) and (ie_k).

- Each expectation state is initialized with transition probabilities $p_{\eta_i \eta_i} = 1$ and $p_{\eta_i \eta_{i+1}} = 0$.

Therefore, for each given expectation state s_{η_i}, the transition probabilities $p_{\eta_i \eta_i}$ and $p_{\eta_i \eta_{i+1}}$ are dynamically altered with each reaction $r \in R$ so that after n_{η_i} time steps the probabilities finally reach $p_{\eta_i \eta_i} = 0$ and $p_{\eta_i \eta_{i+1}} = 1$, which guarantees an expectation state transition that is started with a countdown during which the agent "knows" the current reaction of the environment and transition probabilities remain unmodified (see Figure 5.2). The countdown intervals are included to allow the user to study the agent and the environment in a stable[2] learning-free phase, that is, to see that the agent has completed a learning phase. When the countdown is finished, the environment is set to the next phase state and the agent is back in "learning" mode.

Definition 5.2 (probability change vector)

Let S be a state set, R a reaction set, and $n > 0$. A vector $(v_n)^{(\mu, r)} \in [0,1]^n \subset \mathbb{R}_+^n$ where $0 \le \Sigma_{i=1}^n v_i \le 1$ is called a **probability change vector** of event $r \in R$ in state $s_\mu \in S$. The short form (v_n) can also be used.

Dynamic modification of transition probabilities $p_{\eta_i \eta_i}$ and $p_{\eta_i \eta_{i+1}}$ is achieved through iterative shift of probability values between $p_{\eta_i \eta_i}$ and $p_{\eta_i \eta_{i+1}}$, as defined in the corresponding probability change vector $(v_n)^{(\eta_i, r)}$. In each iteration step k, we have $p_{\eta_i \eta_i}^{(k)} = 1 - \Sigma_{j=1}^k v_j$ and $p_{\eta_i \eta_{i+1}}^{(k)} = \Sigma_{j=1}^k v_j$ for all $k = 1, ..n$ where n is the dimension of the probability change vector. An example is given in Figure 5.3.

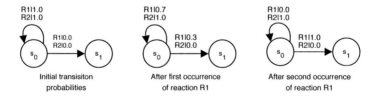

Figure 5.3: Exemplary modification of transition probabilities with probability change vector $(0.3, 0.7)$ for two subsequent occurrences of reaction $R1$

---

[2]The term "stable" means that transition probabilities are not altered while the countdown is running.

The probability change vector allows to model the length and development of the agent's learning process. Data for modeling the various learning processes of a rat can be gathered through rigorous evaluation of video material in order to determine the state transition frequencies for each phase with regard to location, action, and required time to adopt to a new environment phase.

Time-specific processes can be scaled using appropriate values for the probability change vector. Discussions with lecturers of the department of psychology have shown that teaching staff prefer an accelerated, that is, time-scaled, learning behavior because a real-time simulation would most likely exceed the length of a typical lab course.

In the next section, the implementation of the two scenarios is described.

5.1.4 Implementation of Fixed-ratio and Fixed-interval schedules

Since the fixed-interval and fixed-ratio schedule scenario are based on identical 3D assets and an almost identical simulation model, this section covers both scenarios unless indicated otherwise. However, the fixed-ratio schedule scenario is marked as the historical key experiment[3].

Based on video recordings carried out for 2D Flash animations described in Section 5.1.1 and study films "Psychologie des Lernens" by W.F. Angermeier [Ang79], behavior data of a Norwegian rat was gathered and analyzed for all three phases. In accordance with Skinner's theory, the untrained rat started to explore the Skinner box, preferably by navigating close to the walls. Other standard behavior patterns include sniffing and pressing the lever (see Figure 5.4). The causality of pressing the lever and receiving a reward is not immediately comprehended by a rat. The rat must press the lever several times at random and receive a food pellet until it begins to "learn" the causality of the action. Finally, a "trained" rat can be identified by the response frequency. During fixed-ratio schedule, the lever pressing frequency increases as soon as reward delivery is stopped. During fixed-interval schedule, rats first try to receive reward by increasing the lever pressing frequency but later adapt themselves to the time schedule resulting in high frequencies during intervals with reward delivery and low frequencies at other times. The latter result also implies time-awareness and memory capability in rats. Electrical shocks, as applied during the third phase, lead to a rapid decline in the response frequency that ideally reaches 0 Hz.

---

[3]This is owed to the fact that the Replicave framework system can only handle one historical key experiment per historical present.

5.1.4.1   Simulation model

The simulation model has been implemented as a Java applet. Java was chosen because of its capability to trigger the required VRML posture animations via the External Authoring Interface (see Section 2.2.2.2). Since the implementation of a simulation is not the primary scope of this work and due to the complexity of the simulation model required for Skinner's experiments, we will only highlight the most important classes, objects, and methods.

Objects that deal with the applet layout, communication with the VRML scene graph, and the database are instantiated in the main class **Rattensteuerung** that implements the interface EventOutObserver, in which the callback(EventOut *who*, double *when*, Object *which*) method handles EventOut data from the VRML scene graph. VRML nodes with model-specific events are referenced by getNode(). This includes references to nodes communicating animation-related events (*rat*, *SkinnerBox*), position-related data (*rattepos*), time sensor data (*rattimer*), and HUD-related nodes. The latter are interactive controls for the functionalities start/pause simulation, switch to next/previous phase, toggle kymograph display, reset experiment, increase/decrease ratio or time interval[4]. The simulation is initialized with the phase *ALWAYS_PELLETS*. RunFrame() implements the main control for state transitions including a countdown procedure that lasts 20 action steps (see Figure 5.2).

The class **Ratte** is used for controlling the rat's posture properties in the VRML scene graph. It is used for mapping abstract actions on appropriate posture sequences stored in the VRML scene graph of the 3D rat model. This is achieved through stack-based composition of single VRML animations and their processing. Three types of methods are included:

1. Animation composition methods (ComposeLeverStack, ComposeMoveStack, ProcessNextMove)

2. Animation description methods (GetUp, GetDown, TurnLeft, TurnRight, MoveForward, MoveIdle, PushLever)

3. Kymograph-related method SetMark for drawing a mark on the kymograph.

The stack can be filled with string-based command values including *GetDown*, *GetUp*, *MoveForward*, *MoveIdle*, *TurnLeft*, or *TurnRight* that correspond to methods with the same name. Active actions are determined by the function Run-Frame (class Rattensteuerung). Depending on the animation type (lever pressing, idle movement, and movement), the method ComposeLeverStack or Compose-MoveStack is called, by which necessary animations are selected and sorted in the correct order and stored on a stack. Stack processing is initiated by the RunFrame

---

[4]This function depends on the selected scenario.

	Lever	
1 0.1176 0.01569	2 0.0824 0.01569	3 0.1176 0.01569
4 0.0824 0.01569	5 0.0588 0.01569	6 0.0824 0.01569
7 0.1176 0.01569	8 0.0824 0.01569	9 0.1176 0.01569

Field
p(location)
p(sniffing)

Figure 5.4: Field matrix with initial probabilities for default and sniffing postures

function. While the stack contains elements, the next string-based command is read from it and a method with the same name is executed that triggers the corresponding VRML animations. Each VRML animation is terminated with an EventOut message to the callback function in the main class. After receiving an EventOut message, the stack is checked for further animations. In case there are further animations, the callback function is terminated. If the stack is empty, the RunFrame method is called to determine the next action.

The class **State** contains methods required for storage and adjustment of transition probabilities for lever pressing, field-specific presence, and sniffing[5]. The default values for an untrained rat were derived from video material of an untrained rat in a box. Field locations and their initial probabilities are illustrated in Figure 5.4. Variables for these probabilities are assigned in the file State.java.

According to the model design, the transition probabilities depend on the active probability of lever pressing. Therefore, the transition probabilities leading to any of the other ten actions states in $S_\alpha \setminus \{SetMark\} = \{Field(1),...,Field(9),$ $SITUP\_AND\_BEG\}$ are rescaled after each lever pressing action. The updated probability of lever pressing p_0 is considered fixed and the other ten probabilities are linearly rescaled with

$$p_i = p_i(1 - p_0) \, (i = 1, .., 10).$$

Scaled probabilities are calculated by calculateActionProbabilities(float $probPush$-$Lever$).

The agent's decisions are "taken" by a random number generator within the range of given possibilities allowing the rat to "behave" non-deterministically but in

---

[5]The action sniffing describes a sequence of the postures $GetUp$, followed by a sniffing sound and the posture $GetDown$.

Listing 5.1: Calculation of non-deterministic agent decisions in getNextAction()

```
public int getNextAction ()  ...  {
    float random = round (((float)Math.random()));
    float intersum = actionProbabilities [State.PUSH_LEVER];
    if (random < intersum) return State.PUSH_LEVER;
    intersum += actionProbabilities [State.GOTO_FIELD_1];
    if (random < intersum) return State.GOTO_FIELD_1;
    intersum += actionProbabilities [State.GOTO_FIELD_2];
    if (random < intersum) return State.GOTO_FIELD_2;
    ...
    intersum += actionProbabilities [State.GOTO_FIELD_9];
    if (random < intersum) return State.GOTO_FIELD_9;
    intersum += actionProbabilities [State.SITUP_AND_BEG];
    if (random < intersum) return State.SITUP_AND_BEG;
}
```

accordance with Skinner's theory. Random number generation is implemented in getNextAction() (see Listing 5.1).

The class **MarkovModel** contains methods for the conditional execution of expectation state transitions as explained above, based on the environment's reaction to agent-specific actions. The active expectation state is read or set with the methods getCurrentState() and setCurrentState(). The method getNextState() is called from tellLeverResult() and calculates a new state if the lever has been pressed. If the expectation state value remains unchanged, transition probabilities are recalculated or time counters are modified in the case of the fixed-interval scenario. If the new expectation state is different from the current one, the system is set to the new expectation state after enabling or disabling the timer if entering or leaving the fixed-interval scenario. A code excerpt of the method tellLeverResult() is given in Listing 5.2.

The only scenario-specific classes are **RattensteuerungRatio** and **RattensteuerungInterval**, which extend the class Rattensteuerung. The state-specific transition probabilities and probability change vectors are defined in these files/classes.

The class **Schreiber** implements an additional applet window for kymograph output visualization. The applet simulates a paper strip that is continuously moved into a fixed direction (x−axis) and a writing device that draws a mark for every lever pressing action. The values on the y−axis denote the cumulated sum of these actions. Since the y−axis is discrete and limited, the device is reset whenever it reaches a maximal y−value. For convenience, each phase is represented by a special background color over the corresponding time interval (see Figures 5.5 and 5.6).

Listing 5.2: Method tellLeverResult()

```
public void tellLeverResult(int leverResult){
  int nextState = currentState;
  switch (leverResult){
    case GOT_NOTHING:
      nextState =getNextState(matrixNothing[currentState]);
      break;
    case GOT_PELLET:
      nextState = getNextState(matrixPellet[currentState]);
      break;
    case GOT_ELECTRICITY:
      nextState = getNextState(matrixElectricity[currentState]);
      break;
  }
  if (currentState == nextState) {
    try{
      switch (leverResult) {
        case GOT_PELLET:
          if(currentState==2) {
          ... // handle time interval expectation for fixed-
              // interval or probabilities for fixed-ratio
              // scenario
          } else {
          ... // recalculate probabilities
          }
          break;
        case GOT_NOTHING:
          if (currentState==4) {
          ... // handle probabilities for a conditioned agent
          } else {
          ... // recalculate probabilities
          }
          break;
        case GOT_ELECTRICITY:
          ... // recalculate probabilities
          break;
      }
    }
    ... // catch exceptions
  } else {  // state transition
  ... // start or stop timer if entering or leaving
      // fixed-interval scenario state
  currentState = nextState;
  }
}
```

Figure 5.5: Kymograph window in fixed-ratio scenario

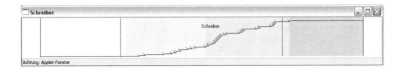

Figure 5.6: Kymograph window in fixed-interval scenario

The class **TimeState** extends the State class by timer-based agent expectations, which are required for the fixed-interval scenario. The class **TimerThread** implements a timer used to measure time intervals in the background.

5.1.4.2   3D assets

Various methods of 3D reconstructive modeling were considered: 3D scanning of an original scene was not feasible because an original historical laboratory did not exist. 3D reconstruction from 2D images was not applicable due to an inadequate amount of image sources. The 3D assets (room, tools, furniture, Skinner box, and the rat) were modeled with the modeling tools Cinema4D, Spazz3D, and VRMLPad.

The sources were filtered with regard to the scenes defined in the storyboard with a focus on didactically or historically important objects. Assets were grouped by animated, non-animated, interactive and non-interactive objects. Since the sources provided only few details about Skinner's historical work environment, a point-wise reconstruction was performed focusing on the floor, walls, a table, the control unit and the Skinner box. The reconstruction of supplementary objects was considered if their lack would result in spatial or logical inconsistencies within the intended scenario. For example, omitting a table due to a missing historical description would render a bare historic room with a Skinner box floating freely in the air causing an irritating inconsistency.

For didactical reasons, the 3D presentation of Skinner's scientific achievement was not limited to a static visualization of the Skinner box as a stand-alone scientific device. Instead, Skinner's laboratory was reconstructed in its historical context.

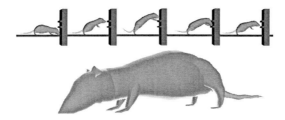

Figure 5.7: Rat model (non-textured) and snapshots of lever pressing animation

Skinner's lab from 1938 did not look like a modern-day laboratory but appears to be an almost rural accommodation with self-made equipment. This aspect has been incorporated by modeling a wooden floor and table, wooden walls, and tools.

The temporal focus was set to 1938 when Skinner's famous article "The Behavior of Organisms" [Ski38] was published. Skinner primarily carried out his experiments with male albino rats (Rattus norvegicus) from various inbred strains in boxes measuring between $10cm \times 20cm$ and $30cm \times 35cm$ at the base. Since no exact measures were given, the reconstruction of the box was derived from photographs of Skinner boxes with rats [Bjo93, Ski84] in relation to the average size (399 mm from head to tail) of an albino Norwegian rat [MA04]. The 3D rat model was designed with the modeling tools Cinema4D, Spazz3D, and VRMLPad based on rat motion sequences in the aforementioned video sources. The smoothed non-textured rat model and development snapshots of the lever pressing animation are depicted in Figure 5.7.

After defining objects that could be confirmed by sources, the rest of the scene was filled by approximating remaining objects in terms of form, position and surface properties in order to reproduce the historical reality with a maximum degree of plausibility. For example, all of Skinner's historic photographs from the 1930's were black and white. With the exception of the rats, there was hardly any information about the color of the equipment in use. Various materials were investigated focusing on their historical development, regional distribution and color. As Garner [Gar80] and Watson [Wat79] point out, walnut, oak and pine were the preferred lumbers for plank and furniture installations in the Eastern and Mid-Western regions of the USA in the early 20th century. Hence, the scene was equipped with corresponding textures. Similar considerations were made for the choice of other materials. For example, the frame of the remote control unit for reinforcement delivery was reconstructed using a black Bakelite texture. Figure 5.8 illustrates a screenshot of the replicated Skinner laboratory and experiment.

The HUD elements are based on the framework's HUD library with modifications to suit the experiment's interaction requirements.

Figure 5.8: Virtual rat in the Skinner box, kymograph, and food dispenser

5.1.5 Conclusion

Two historical scenarios of the Skinner experiment on operant conditioning have been reconstructed in virtual 3D laboratories and have been implemented as interactive 3D experiments including a virtual rat controlled by a non-deterministic behavior model. The model allows reversible execution of the experiments with interactive user control and provides visual feedback.

The amount of lines of code (LoC) and person-months spent on the implementation of these two experiments are given in Table 5.2. The relatively large amount of person-months spent on the development of the 3D rat model is mainly due to manual optimization of the VRML code. As mentioned in Chapter 4, the VRML file export filters of the 3D modeling suites generated VRML code with redundant polygons (software-based triangularization) and had to be manually post-processed. Furthermore, VRML Script nodes for animation control had to be added manually in text-based VRML editors.

The present implementations show that the combination of VRML and Java is a feasible platform for the replication of classical psychological experiments in web-based virtual environments. However, even on high-performance PC workstations, synchronization issues were sometimes detected during rat animation sequences. The issues could be resolved if the amount of animation sequences in the rat model file was reduced. Hence, the animation complexity of the 3D rat model presented here may not be increased further.

Software description (programming language)	LoC	Cost (person-months)
Simulation model (Java)	3k	5
3D rat model (VRML)	14k	20
Other 3D assets (VRML)	15k	6

Table 5.2: Skinner experiments: Lines of code and cost (person-months) of software programming

A more detailed simulation model might include advanced features, such as an 8-neighborhood topology for visualizing rat movement (that is, movements to the NE, SW, SE, and NW), increased field resolution, and additional actions and postures. Another advantage of using a discrete time and state based simulation model and a Java applet is the possibility to pass parameters, offering a wide range of applications: users could stop the experiment and load personalized time/state parameters from the database. Advanced learners may experiment with rats extremely sensible to conditioning by supplying additional rat profiles with different transition probabilities and probability change vectors. Furthermore, additional levers and stimuli might be added. The Java-based Skinner experiments have been implemented in German only. A database connector was not implemented for performance reasons. However, this would allow recording of simulation based data with regard to a detailed analysis and optimization of the proposed simulation model.

5.2 Tolman: Construction of cognitive maps

Important and early support for a cognitive view of instrumental learning was provided by work carried out by Edward C. Tolman (1886-1959) and others in the 1920s, 30s, and 40s. At the time, many behaviorists thought of instrumental learning as a strict stimulus-response (S-R) connection. Tolman conducted several classical rat experiments including studies that involved maze running. He examined the role of reinforcers in the learning process of rats looking for a way through complex mazes [Mie98, p.193ff.].

5.2.1 Key experiment: Cognitive maps

Tolman used several maze types including the so-called T-maze, a maze that consisted of a starting point, a goal, and a sequence of basic T-shaped elements, of which the letter's base represents an entrance with a one-way-door. After passing through the door, the subject must decide whether to turn left or right. Both alternative ways are covered by removable curtains, one hiding a "dead

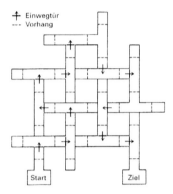

Figure 5.9: Maze layout used in Tolman's experiment [Mie98, p.193]

end" and the other hiding a further entrance or the goal. Figure 5.9 illustrates the original 2D layout.

The first group of (hungry) rats was rewarded with food at the goal. The experiment was conducted over a 16-day period during which the rats were able to find the correct way to the goal with a continuously decreasing amount of errors, that is, entering a "dead end". The control group did not receive any reward at the goal during the first 10 days. Instead, they were allowed to wander freely through the maze. On the 11th day, Tolman started to provide food as a reinforcer and found that, on the 12th day, most rats would find the correct way in the shortest time possible.

These experiments led to the theory of latent learning that, in contrary to the S-R theory, states that learning can also occur in the absence of an obvious reward. Moreover, Tolman postulated that the rats in the second group had developed a cognitive map of the maze's spatial structure [TH30].

5.2.1.1   3D assets

Based on the historical maze layout (see Figure 5.9), a 3D maze was modeled with a start box, a sequence of T-shaped elements, interactive curtains, and a goal box (see Figure 5.10), each of which was implemented as a VRML PROTO. In order to provide a minimal amount of global landmarks, the maze was situated in a white-colored room. Object ceilings were made semi-transparent.

The 3D assets were produced during a virtual reality study project using the modeling tools VRMLPad and Spazz3D.

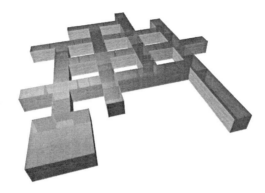

Figure 5.10: Reconstructed 3D maze

5.2.1.2 Interaction model

Although the historical experiment was carried out with rats, it is unlikely that users will observe the experiment for a time span of 12 or 16 days. Since Tolman's theory was formulated with regard to both rats and humans and in order to increase the user's sensation during the experiment, the user was given the role of a subject.

One-way doors, curtains, and the reward are interactive objects. If a curtain is clicked, an animation is started visualizing an opening curtain. By clicking on the reward, the instruction text is switched and the user receives an information that the experiment has been terminated. The default HUD is used.

5.2.1.3 Implementation

The implementation is stored in the folder `tmaze` using the above-mentioned 3D assets. Each "open curtain" event triggers a PHP script (`dbanbindung.php`) by which current values of *labrun, session, time, baseID,* and *user* are added to the table `tolmanPath` of the VirtLab database.

The random value *labrun* is generated once per visit and allows to filter user generated data on a per-visit basis. User-specific data sets can be identified by their session id (*session*) or the optional username (*user*). In addition, a time stamp (*time*) is stored. The identifier (*baseID*) denotes the location and type of a curtain. Curtains covering doors are numbered sequentially following the unique path from the start to the goal, starting with index 1. Curtains covering a "dead end" are indexed likewise, starting with index 50. The last curtain has index 100.

Figure 5.11 illustrates an exemplary data set of a maze run.

labrun	session	time	baseID
1616649443	nne49veqannj69et6g4onpv414	2006-05-24 10:28:35	1
1616649443	nne49veqannj69et6g4onpv414	2006-05-24 10:28:42	50
1616649443	nne49veqannj69et6g4onpv414	2006-05-24 10:28:45	2
1616649443	nne49veqannj69et6g4onpv414	2006-05-24 10:28:52	3
1616649443	nne49veqannj69et6g4onpv414	2006-05-24 10:28:55	52
1616649443	nne49veqannj69et6g4onpv414	2006-05-24 10:29:00	4
1616649443	nne49veqannj69et6g4onpv414	2006-05-24 10:29:04	5
1616649443	nne49veqannj69et6g4onpv414	2006-05-24 10:29:08	54
1616649443	nne49veqannj69et6g4onpv414	2006-05-24 10:29:11	6
1616649443	nne49veqannj69et6g4onpv414	2006-05-24 10:29:14	7
1616649443	nne49veqannj69et6g4onpv414	2006-05-24 10:29:19	8
1616649443	nne49veqannj69et6g4onpv414	2006-05-24 10:29:22	57
1616649443	nne49veqannj69et6g4onpv414	2006-05-24 10:29:25	9
1616649443	nne49veqannj69et6g4onpv414	2006-05-24 10:29:30	58
1616649443	nne49veqannj69et6g4onpv414	2006-05-24 10:29:32	10
1616649443	nne49veqannj69et6g4onpv414	2006-05-24 10:29:42	11
1616649443	nne49veqannj69et6g4onpv414	2006-05-24 10:29:45	12
1616649443	nne49veqannj69et6g4onpv414	2006-05-24 10:29:50	13
1616649443	nne49veqannj69et6g4onpv414	2006-05-24 10:29:55	62
1616649443	nne49veqannj69et6g4onpv414	2006-05-24 10:29:59	14
1616649443	nne49veqannj69et6g4onpv414	2006-05-24 10:30:03	100

Figure 5.11: Recorded dataset of maze experiment

5.2.2 Landmark experiment

The discovery of cognitive maps implied further research including the role of landmarks in visual navigation. In their paper entitled "The Role of Global and Local Landmarks in Virtual Environment Navigation", S.D. Steck and H.A. Mallot describe an experiment that was performed to scrutinize the role of global and local landmarks for the acquisition of route knowledge in a virtual environment [SM00].

Subjects had to navigate through a virtual urban environment. In the first part of the experiment both local and global landmarks were present, and the results showed that both were used in the navigational decision task. In the second part of the experiment the influence of partial information on navigation was examined using the same scenery as in the first experiment with three different lighting conditions. In the scenario using "night" lighting condition, only local landmarks were visualized. In the "dawn" lighting scenario, only global landmarks without textures were visualized. The "default" lighting condition from the first experiment was used as a control condition.

Based on the results, Steck and Mallot postulated that participants have access to both types of landmark information.

In his BSc. thesis entitled "Konzeption und Implementation eines Landmarken-Experiments zur Integration in Replicave" [Pan05] A. Pankov described the design and implementation of a VRML-based urban virtual environment with two lighting conditions, inspired by the experiment by Steck and Mallot. The first "dawn" lighting condition focused on local landmarks, while the other represented the "default" lighting condition with both global and local landmarks. The virtual environment was not intended to be an exact reproduction of the virtual environment by Steck and Mallot. However, it was integrated into the Replicave system as an example of contemporary research activity related to Tolman's historical experiment.

5.2.2.1 3D assets

Pankov's implementation included all required 3D assets for the visualization of an urban scenery. It featured less global landmarks, the distances between adjacent streets are shorter, and the barriers marking dead ends are located closer to the main path, as compared to the original environment described by Steck and Mallot.

These 3D assets were used in the Replicave implementation after slight modifications with regard to file size optimization.

5.2.2.2 Interaction model

As in the experiment of Steck and Mallot, the user is in the subject's role. Both start and goal area were marked by a special landmark, that is, a blue post box. At the beginning of the experiment, the user is instructed to walk around and to look for a second blue post box. If he has found the second box, he is instructed to return to the start point. If the user has returned to the start point after finding the goal, he is informed that the experiment has been finished successfully. The sensor's enter or exit event are to be monitored and recorded.

Since the user is situated in a virtually "open environment" outside closed rooms, an interactive navigation function was provided allowing the user to return to the framework system at any time.

Due to the simplicity of the model, we omit an abstract representation of an interaction model.

5.2.2.3 Implementation

The implementations are stored in the folders landmark_1 ("dawn" lighting condition) and landmark_2 (default lighting condition). Viewpoint definition, HUD-specific data, and proximity sensors are defined in the file index.php, from which the main 3D asset file (village.wrl) is included through a VRML Inline node.

The volumetric space around each post box is covered by an invisible proximity sensor. With minor exceptions, both VRML worlds share the same geometric urban model allowing the use of identical position and size values for the ProximitySensors in both scene graphs.

Four event types are monitored, as described in Table 5.3. For any monitored event, the current status number (*status*), time stamp (*time*), and session id (*session*) are stored in the tables tolmanLandmark1 and tolmanLandmark2, respectively. The PHP script dbscript.php provides the database connectivity.

Since the experiment required three instruction levels, the Messagebox PROTO of the default HUD was extended by a third string type parameter *string2* in which the third instruction text is stored. The extended PROTO definition is stored in the experiment's folder (GUIObjects3D.wrl).

Figures 5.12 and 5.13 depict screenshots of the implementation.

Status	Event	Sensor	Description
0	exitTime	ProxSensorStart	User leaves starting area.
1	enterTime	ProxSensorStart	User re-enters starting area without entering goal area.
2	enterTime	ProxSensorEnd	User enters goal area.
3	enterTime	ProxSensorStart	User re-enters starting area after having entered goal area.

Table 5.3: Status descriptions (landmark experiment)

Figure 5.12: Landmark experiment ("dawn" lighting condition)

Figure 5.13: Landmark experiment (default lighting condition)

5.2.3 Conclusion

The replication of Tolman's historical experiment showed that the user sensation should be considered for applicable role assignment and the resulting interaction model. As a result, relatively few 3D assets were required. Event monitoring and recording allow user-specific tempo-spatial path reconstruction from the decision data stored in the database (see Figure 5.11).

The landmark experiment represents an implementation of a non-historical experiment based on existing 3D assets. The modular design of the Replicave framework system allowed an integration of interactive sensors and a database connector with only minor modifications of the original code. As in the historical maze experiment, the sensors and scripts provide a technical means to generate data sets that allow decision monitoring and delta time measurements. Based on this technique, the sensor grid might be refined further by psychological experts to scrutinize navigational decision tasks at a higher resolution.

5.3 Ebbinghaus: The forgetting curve

It was Hermann Ebbinghaus (1850-1909) who introduced the scientific methodology of experimentation to the study of "higher" cognitive processes. His experiments started in 1878 and were continued during the years 1879/80 and 1883/84. The research was carried out at his home in Barmen/Germany and culminated in the book "Über das Gedächnis: Untersuchungen zur experimentellen

Psychologie"[Ebb85] published in 1885. The publication is considered a turning point in the history of psychology, because the processes of learning and retention were scrutinized while they occurred (and not afterwards) and because they were gained through the new methodology of experimentation, which confirmed Ebbinghaus' reputation as the "founder of scientific memory research" [Tra86].

Ebbinghaus measured the rate of decay of memory and expressed this in a mathematical function, the so-called forgetting function. Its graphical representation is called the forgetting curve.

5.3.1   Key experiment: The forgetting curve

Ebbinghaus assumed that the process of committing information to the memory involved the formation of new associations that would be strengthened through repetition. In order to observe this process with information that would not have any previous associations, he prepared 2291 paper cards with so-called nonsense syllables, that is, consonant-vowel-consonant (CVC) trigrams. The cards were used as stimulus material [Ebb85].

For the experiment, in which Ebbinghaus was the sole participant, he randomly selected a sequence of these syllables and denoted them. The length of sequences varied. During the years 1879/80, between 72 and 150 syllables were used. Once a sequence was determined, Ebbinghaus learned it by reading it aloud using, among other time-measuring devices, a metronome set to 150 beats per minute until he could reproduce the entire sequence. His experiment included the following retention tests:

- Free recall: Describes the attempt to recall the syllables of a studied sequence, regardless of their order.

- Serial recall: Describes the attempt to recall the syllables of a studied sequence in the correct order.

- Recognition: Describes the attempt to recognize studied syllables from a given list of syllables.

Measuring the memory was accomplished by the *percent savings* quantifier that was considered to deliver the most sensitive indication of a residual effect of previous learning, as compared to simply counting the amount of correctly recalled syllables after a retention interval. The measure was defined as:

$$percent\ savings := \frac{n_2}{n_1} \cdot 100\%$$

For various predefined retention intervals, the mean average of the amount of repetitions required after the retention interval (n_2) is divided by the mean average of the amount of repetitions required to learn the original sequence for the first time (n_1).

The results acquired through the serial recall test procedure over a period of a month and the *percent savings* measurement is known as Ebbinghaus' forgetting function. The experiment indicated "rapid forgetting" during the first few days. Thereafter, "forgetting", that is, the amount of required rehearsals, increased only slowly.

Replication focus

Ebbinghaus' long-term experiment needs to be carried out regularly by the same subject under similar conditions in real-time, that is, over a period of one month before results can be calculated and demonstrated. Even the measurement of the first three historical retention intervals would take at least an hour.

Ebbinghaus was both: researcher and subject. A web-based replication of the experiment would strongly depend on unknown conditions at the user's (remote) location, a user who is in the subject's role could generate data that might not correspond with Ebbinghaus' findings and rather irritate the user. Furthermore, it is questionable if any user would be disciplined enough to conduct the experiment as regularly as required. Hence, it is most likely that a user learns faster about the experiment through classical media, such as written or spoken text, than through an interactive real-time replication of the experiment with more than 72 syllable cards.

Therefore, the replication of Ebbinghaus' historical key experiment focuses primarily on the serial recall test procedure with only ten cards serving as stimulus material, which allows a user to take Ebbinghaus' role and to participate in the experiment in a reasonable time interval while heeding the demand of a historically contextualized visualization.

5.3.1.1 3D assets

Photographs or detailed descriptions of the interior of Ebbinghaus' private house were not available. 3D assets were replicated to resemble a room in a private house located in a German town around 1880. The room contains a desk and a pack of cards. A historical metronome was extracted from a reconstruction by E. Süselbeck [Süs03] and converted to a VRML PROTO.

Other assets, such as furniture, a firesite, and a couch were reconstructed to create an authentic ambiance. An image of a historical market place is visible through the room's exterior window to underline the location's urban setting. An animated hourglass was modeled as a time-measuring device. With the exception of the metronome, the 3D assets were produced by students during a virtual reality study project using the modeling tools VRMLPad and Spazz3D.

Figure 5.14: Sütterlin font texture (inverted image)

Syllable visualization is achieved through a modified version of the Text3D PROTO (see Section 4.5.8) with a prerendered bitmapped Sütterlin font, a historical font used by Ebbinghaus. Since Sütterlin is no default system font, a VRML compliant bitmap was generated from a free true type font[6]. A font table was visualized with the freeware tool Bitmap Font Generator[7] and stored as an image file. Utilizing the image processing software GIMP[8], the bitmapped letters were isolated from the background and colored in white[9]. The resulting font texture file was stored as a PNG image file (`suetterlin.png`) with transparent background (see Figure 5.14).

5.3.1.2   Interaction/simulation model

At the beginning of the experiment, an interactive pack of cards is placed on the desk. If clicked, the cards are animated as if they were shuffled to underline the randomness of the syllable sequence. Then, a complete sequence of ten cards, each of which displaying a (randomly generated) CVC trigram, is arranged on the desktop. The cards are displayed for an interval of ten seconds before they are turned around. At the beginning of this presentation the hourglass is turned around visualizing the presentation time interval of ten seconds after which the cards are turned around again.

The user is asked to enter the syllables he recalls in ascending order. Each character is displayed in the same font as used for the syllables. Syllable input finished by pressing the Enter key. Then, the input is compared with the original syllable before feedback (*"correct"* / *"wrong"*) is provided.

If the user clicks on the card pack or on any of the presented cards, the ten drawn

---

[6]http://www.suetterlinschrift.de/Lese/SUETTER.TTF [Accessed 17 May 2006]

[7]http://www.angelcode.com/products/bmfont [Accessed 17 May 2006]

[8]http://www.gimp.org/ [Accessed 17 May 2006]

[9]The white (neutral) color attribute is required for the Text3D PROTO since the rendered font color is determined by a colored light source at runtime.

cards are turned around and the sequence is presented for another ten seconds before the cards are turned around again. The latter interaction should also be possible during syllable recall, that is, the user can interrupt the recall process when realizing that he can not correctly rememorize a syllable. Each syllable recall attempt is to be recorded in the VirtLab database.

Due to the simplicity of the model, we omit an abstract representation.

5.3.1.3   Implementation

The implementation is stored in the folder font_suetterlin. The main asset file is index.wrl. The visualization uses the default lab room HUD layout. The hourglass interval (ten seconds) is set through the *cycleInterval* parameter of the HourGlass PROTO instantiation. The card pack's geometric model and control logic are stored in the file cards.wrl.inc.php. This includes card animation, random CVC trigram generation, and feedback localization. Character input is based on a modified version of the Text3D PROTO.

A screenshot of the historical Ebbinghaus experiment is given in Figure 5.15.

If a user enters a recalled sequence, both random and recalled syllables are stored in the tables ebbHistSuett (historical font) and ebbHistTimes (modern font, see Section 5.3.2), together with the session id and a timestamp. The database connection is provided by the PHP script ebb_dbscript.php.

5.3.1.4   The concept keyboard

A concept keyboard is a flat board that contains an (n×m)-matrix of touch sensors. It is connected to a PC via a hardware input interface, usually the USB interface. Utilizing a keyboard-specific driver and mapping software, each sensor or groups of sensors can be mapped to letters, letter groups, or actions. Keyboard layouts are defined by overlay sheets that are placed on the sensor matrix.

Since the Sütterlin font is historical and most users are likely to be unfamiliar with it, a Sütterlin font layout and sheet overlay was generated for an Intellisys ConceptKeyboard. This was done to prove the feasibility of integrating hardware devices other than standard mouse or keyboard into the system. However, the price of such hardware devices must be considered as very high.

5.3.2   Modified key experiment with contemporary font

The historical laboratory was copied and published as a separate laboratory. For better readability, the historical Sütterlin font was replaced with a contemporary Times font that corresponds with the font on the input device, that is, a standard PC keyboard. All font texture URL references were changed to the new texture file name font.png. The files are stored in the folder font_modern. A screenshot of the Ebbinghaus experiment with a contemporary font is given in Figure 5.16.

Figure 5.15: Historical Ebbinghaus experiment with Sütterlin font

Figure 5.16: Historical Ebbinghaus experiment with Times font

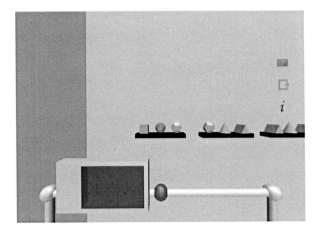

Figure 5.17: Ebbinghaus experiment (Letter-free version)

5.3.3 Letter-free implementation

In his master's thesis "Erstellung eines VRML-basierten Systems zum Gedächtnis-experiment von Hermann Ebbingshaus als Schlüsselexperiment der Psychologie unter Berücksichtigung verschiedenener Nutzergruppen" E. Süselbeck describes the design and implementation of a letter-free version of the Ebbinghaus experiment [Süs03]. Süselbeck's implementation uses geometric shapes of different colors as a replacement for single letters. The random CVC syllables are generated from a set of six consonants (tetrahedron, dodecahedron, cube, cuboid, extruded triangle, bipyramid) and five vowels (cylinder, sphere, cone, ellipsoid, bicone). A sequence of twenty syllables is generated. Each syllable is placed on a shelf that is attached to a wall. In front of the shelves, a transport rig allows the user to navigate along the wall and to select syllables interactively from a virtual keyboard that serves as input device (see Figure 5.17).

The files are stored in the folder noalpha. Each sequence of recalled geometric objects is stored in the table abcfrei_Versuchsablauf of the VirtLab database. Once the user has completed the input of a recalled sequence, the room is reloaded and correctly recalled "syllables" are visualized as a feedback. The integration of Süselbeck's assets required additional localized data, HUD integration and marginal modifications in the database connection script abcfrei_dbscript.php. 3D assets and the interaction model are described in Süselbeck's thesis.

Süselbeck's letter-free implementation was intended primarily as a stand-alone version for special user groups, such as illiterate users. Since navigational information about the location of this laboratory is provided in text-based form within the framework system, the stand-alone implementation appears to be better suited for illiterate users. However, the letter-free version was included as it underlines the scientific methodology used by Ebbinghaus.

5.3.4 Conclusion

The replication of Ebbinghaus' historical experiment showed the combined potential of software-based text rendering capability (Text3D PROTO with character input and historical font visualization) and a corresponding hardware-specific input device (concept keyboard). The alternative implementation, which is using a contemporary font, was intended to provide a user-friendly replication with regard to visual stimuli and standard input devices.

The letter-free implementation of Ebbinghaus' experiment showed the advantage of a modular and open architecture of the framework system allowing an easy integration of existing 3D content.

5.4 Sperling: Iconic memory

In the late 1950s, George Sperling began to investigate the sensory register. He conducted a key experiment that lead to the discovery of the capacity and duration of a short term visual memory, which was later called the iconic memory [BZ03, Mie98]. In 1960, Sperling published the paper "The information available in brief visual presentations" that describes the key experiment and its findings [Spe60]. In fact, Sperling's paper describes a sequence of seven experiments, all of which deal with subjects who were required to report letters of briefly exposed lettered stimuli. Since the entire sequence of the experiments lead to Sperling's findings, they are usually referred to as "Sperling's iconic memory experiment".

5.4.1 Key experiment: Iconic memory

During Sperling's iconic memory experiment, groups of nine or twelve letters were presented to participants for 50 msecs, using a tachistoscope[10]. Regardless of the amount of letters presented, the participants were found to be able to nearly always recall four or five (35-40%) of these, even if the exposure time was increased to 500 msecs.

To answer the question whether this was due to a problem of brief capacity or brief duration, Sperling modified the experimental setup. Again, three rows of three or four letters were presented together with sound signals of a different frequency. A high tone indicated the participants to recall the top row, a medium tone the middle row, and a low tone the bottom row, respectively. The rows

---

[10]A tachistoscope is a device for the brief display of visual stimuli.

were displayed for 50 msecs. After another 50 msecs the participants heard the signal that indicated which row to recall. In the latter case, the participants were excellent at recalling all four items in a row. If the signal was given 300 msecs after the presentation of the rows, the participants could recall about two letters. If the signal was given one second after the presentation of the rows, the participants could recall as many letters as in the earlier experiment, which was conducted without any acoustic signal.

Sperling concluded that the sensory register has a relatively large capacity, but a short duration span of less than 300 msecs, also known as the individual span of immediate-memory [Mie98].

5.4.1.1 Existing 2D replication

In their master's thesis entitled "Zur Reliabilität und Validität von Online-Experimenten. Multimediale Replikation eines Gedächnispsychologischen Experiments (Sperling, 1960) als Lerneinheit für die Weiterbildung", F. Bick and K. Zeppenfeld presented a complete 2D web-based learning unit of Sperling's iconic memory experiment, implemented in Macromedia Flash [BZ03]. Bick's and Zeppenfeld's application included a replication of the seven experiments described above utilizing an interaction logic based on Flash technology. Flash was used to ensure the required client-sided timing precision for the brief exposure of the visual stimuli.

With the permission of the authors, an integration of the existing 2D Flash application into a new 3D lab environment was realized.

5.4.1.2 3D assets

3D asset reproduction focused on the experiment's historical location and apparatus. Sperling conducted preceding experiments at the Bell Telephone laboratories [Spe60, pp.24-25]. From 1957 to 1959, he was a visiting research assistant in Psychology at Harvard University, where he also used the laboratory and tachistoscope of Jerome S. Bruner [Spe60, p.1]. Despite the preceding experiments and laboratories, it can be assumed that the key experiment described in the above mentioned paper, took place at Harvard University. Hence, the laboratory was reconstructed following the design of a campus room, equipped with furniture and a tachistoscope.

The room's interior was modeled according to one of the few published photographs of Sperling, in which the psychologist is situated in front of a file cabinet and a working desk (see Figures 5.18 and 5.19). The 3D assets, including the tachistoscope (see Figure 5.20), were produced during a virtual reality study project using the modeling tools VRMLPad and Spazz3D.

Figure 5.18: Sperling: Historical photograph [Spe06]

Figure 5.19: Reconstructed room

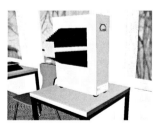

Figure 5.20: Reconstructed tachistoscope

5.4.1.3   Implementation

The third-party Flash animation was available in binary form only. Since it included an internal interaction logic, it was processed as a black-box application.
As mentioned in Chapter 2, Flash-based textures are not supported by the current
version of the VRML plug-in. In order to avoid irritation through media discontinuity between native 3D (VRML) and 2D (Flash) content, a special visual effect
was implemented.

Sperling used a binocular tachistoscope. Hence, the laboratory's interior is not
seen by a subject while using the tachistoscope appropriately. Therefore, a new
"tachistoscope view" was defined, in which the 2D content is embedded in a full-
screen HTML frameset and displayed in the center of the screen. The surrounding
area is black imitating the effect of looking into a binocular tachistoscope. The
experiment is started by clicking on the interactive tachistoscope apparatus. If
activated, the user's sensation of remaining in a 3D world is sustained by moving
the camera's viewpoint into the binocular eyepieces, as in a fly-through animation.

In "tachistoscope view", an interactive escape button is visualized at the lower
right side of the screen allowing the user to return to the original 3D view. The
button was implemented due to the animation's black-box design that prevented
the addition of new or the modification of existing interactive control elements.

In VRML-based rendering mode, this implementation uses the default lab room
HUD layout. The experiment's files are stored in the 1960_iconicmem folder.

5.4.2   Preceding/Succeeding experiments

Replicave does not feature any implementation of preceding or succeeding experiments in the context of Sperling's discovery of the iconic memory.

5.4.3   Conclusion

The implementation of Sperling's iconic memory experiment was achieved through
a combination of a geometrically reconstructed 3D laboratory room and an existing 2D Flash learning unit. Media discontinuities were circumvented by an
animated viewpoint change that intends to trick the user's perception by zoom-
ing in on a 3D object and switching to 2D-based rendering. The implementation of Sperling's experiment shows the feasibility of integrating closed-sourced
third-party 2D-only content if existing content can be visualized without media
discontinuities.

5.5 Duncker: Functional fixedness

Karl Duncker (1903-1940) was a researcher in the field of cognitive psychology. His studies dealt with problem solving - or productive thinking, as Duncker himself called it. *Functional fixedness* describes the ability (or inability) to solve a problem in a creative manner by using an object out of its original context.

In 1926 Duncker received an M.A. from Clark University[11] with his thesis, "An Experimental and Theoretical Study of Productive Thinking (Solving of Comprehensible Problems)", which was published the same year under a slightly modified title in *Pedagogical Seminary* [Dun26]. In his thesis, he presents problem solving tasks, including the candle problem.

5.5.1 Key experiment: The candle problem

The candle problem describes the following initial situation: a candle and a box containing pushpins, matches, and other objects are placed on a table. The subjects are asked to light the candle and to fix it on a near-by pinboard that is attached to a wall so that the candle does not drip on the table below.

The solution to this problem is to empty the box, use the pushpins to tack the box against the wall, and to place the candle in the box in an upright position. Alternatively, the box is emptied, the candle placed into the box, and the box (including the candle) attached to the wall.

Subjects tended to have difficulties finding the solution as long as they conceived of the box's function as a container for pushpins. The functional fixedness was overcome if a subject comprehended that the box's side or ground panels could be used as a base for the candle [Mie98, pp.220ff.].

Although the historical experiment and its scientific theory is well documented [Dun26, Dun45], limited information is available about the architectural environment in which the experiment was originally conducted. Since Duncker was at Clark University in 1926, it is most likely that the experiment was originally conducted in rooms at this location.

The nature of the experiment is ideally suited for 3D implementation: Various objects are presented on a table, some of them must be "taken", moved through a 3D space and put down at another location.

5.5.1.1 3D assets

Due to missing data on the historical architectural environment, the setting was reconstructed by focusing on essential objects: a medium-sized room equipped with a chair, a pinboard, and a table. On top of the table are a candle, four

---

[11]The Clark University is located in Worcester, Massachusetts (USA).

matches, three pushpins, three paper clips, and a box. For plausibility reasons, the room was filled with additional objects unrelated to the experiment: a locker, a plant, a lamp, and some decorative desktop objects. All objects and the room's interior design were designed to resemble a style from an arbitrary small US university office around 1926.

All non-animated 3D assets were produced by students during a virtual reality study project using the modeling tools VRMLPad and Spazz3D. Attention was paid to visualizing only technical inventions (lamp), furniture designs and surface textures whose historical existence could be assumed.

5.5.1.2 Interaction model

To achieve a high degree of interactivity under the constrain of 2D input devices (mouse and keyboard), a "click-and-use" control was intended for the implementation. The PlaneSensor node in VRML97 can only be used to drag an object along a hyperplane (that is, a 2D subplane), which is optionally limited with an upper and lower width/height boundary. However, this would not provide free object movement in three dimensions, which is needed for the experiment (for example, when objects are taken out of the box and are placed elsewhere).

Therefore, a list of discrete positions was determined for each object. The user can operate objects by selecting an *active* object and *use* it with another *passive* object in a predefined context (see Table 5.4).

		Active objects					
		candle	match	pushpin	paper clip	box	table/ pinboard
	candle	put up-right	light	-	-	-	-
Passive objects	match	-	-	-	-	-	-
	pushpin	-	-	-	-	-	-
	paper clip	-	-	-	-	-	-
	box	put into	put into	put into, pin through	put into	-	-
	table	put on	put on	put on	put on	put on	-
	pinboard	-	-	pin onto	-	hold on	-

Table 5.4: Duncker's candle problem: Predefined object contexts

Considering both discrete object locations and the predefined object contexts, the interaction model can be defined as a finite state machine (FSM). Each set of discrete object positions defines a unique state, the selection of a pair of active and passive objects defines an input action, and the interaction context (see

Table 5.4) defines the transition conditions. In order to estimate the complexity of the FSM, we analyze the number of required object positions, the initial state, the final state, and selected transitions.

In the initial state, the box contains all the paper clips and pushpins and is located on the table. The candle and the matches are lying on the table next to the box.

Various actions lead to the final state. Before the box can be attached to the pinboard, the box has to be located on the table and must not contain any matches, pushpins, or paper clips since these would hinder the candle from being fixed securely on the bottom of the box. To attach the box to the pinboard, the box has to be fixed by at least two pushpins. The box is attached correctly once the user has performed three sequential actions ("attachment sequence") in the following order and without any other intermediate actions.

1. The box must be picked up and held against the pinboard.

2. The box must be attached to the pinboard by one pushpin.

3. The box must be fixed with a second pushpin.

If any of the objects is not operated in the correct order, all objects involved "fall down", which means that the box, the candle, or the pushpin(s) are reset to positions on the table. That is, the empty box is put back on the table and, if affected, the pushpins are located on the table, and the candle is located next to them in its original unlit state.

The candle problem is successfully solved if the actions defined in the "attachment sequence" are executed correctly **and** if the candle is located inside the box, regardless of whether the candle is lit or not at this position.

Furthermore, the following constraints and/or conditions have to be met:

- Objects with more than one position are the candle, the matches, the pushpins, the paper clips, and the box. Each of these objects can be put on the table and - with the exception of the box - all can be put into the box if the box is located on top of the table.

- The candle can either lie unlit on the table, be placed in an upright position on the table, or be placed into the box, if the box is located on the table or is safely attached to the pinboard.

- The candle can be lit with a match in any upright position.

- Unless the "attachment sequence" is in progress, any of the three pushpins can be tacked directly to the pinboard.

- The candle can only be placed into the box if the box is empty. Otherwise, we assume that the candle is not fixed securely.

- If the candle is located inside the box, no other objects can be put into box. Allowing this would require adding further object positions in order to prevent object intersection and would increase the model's complexity.

Having defined an initial and final state as well as interaction constraints, a specific interaction model can be developed. Let P_{object} denote the set of different positions for each object. There are $card(P_{candle} \times P_{match1} \times \ldots \times P_{match4} \times P_{pushpin1} \times \ldots \times P_{pushpin3} \times P_{paperclip1} \times \ldots \times P_{paperclip3} \times P_{box}) = 3 \cdot 2^4 \cdot 4^3 \cdot 2^3 \cdot 2 = 49152$ combinations of possible object positions.

Considering the constraints mentioned, the required combinations of object positions for a visual implementation can be determined by monitoring the position of the box:

1. If the box is located on the table and contains at least one object other than a candle, there remain two positions for the candle: it can lie on the table or be placed upright on the table. Hence, there are $2 \cdot 2^4 \cdot 3^3 \cdot 2^3 \cdot 1 = 6912$ object combinations.

2. If the box is located on the table and is empty, the candle can be placed upright in the box (1 object combination).

3. During the "attachment sequence", the box is held against the pinboard and fixed by at most three pushpins. Here, the candle is located either on the table (two positions) or in the box. All matches and paperclips remain on the table. Hence, there are $3 \cdot 1 \cdot 2^3 \cdot 1 \cdot 1 = 24$ possible object combinations, including those of the final state.

Summarizing, $6912 + 1 + 24 = 6937$ combinations of object positions are required under the mentioned constraints. The majority of the possible combinations can be excluded by the constraint that the box must be empty during and after the "attachment sequence".

From a user's perspective, Duncker's candle problem is basically solved in three steps:

1. Remove all objects from the box.

2. Attach the empty box to the pinboard.

3. Place the candle in an upright position in the box.

However, steps 2 and 3 can be executed in an arbitrary order. We use a UML statechart diagram to draft the FSM. Since VRML97 is not object-oriented, UML diagram types that refer to object-oriented patterns appeared to be less suited if code has to be derived from the model at a later point. Although UML activity diagrams seem to be suited for modeling as well, it is questionable, with regard to the amount of possible activities and object positions, how complex the model may become and whether an implementation could be derived from it easily.

The three above mentioned solution steps can be expressed through nine super states:

- State 0: The box is located on the table and is not empty (including the initial state).

- State 0': The box is located on the table and contains the candle.

- State 0": The box is located on the table and is empty.

- State 1: The empty box is held against the pinboard.

- State 1': The box contains the candle and is held against the pinboard.

- State 2: The empty box is attached to the pinboard with one pushpin.

- State 2': The box contains the candle and is attached to the pinboard with one pushpin.

- State 3: The empty box is attached to the pinboard with two pushpins.

- State 3': The box contains the candle and is attached to the pinboard with two pushpins (final state).

Using these nine super states, a UML statechart diagram was developed (see Figure 5.21). If possible, both events and actions were denoted and conditions were formulated to facilitate the implementation. The action */operate objects* describes object position changes that do not lead to any super state transition.

For convenience, only the super states were denoted. By this, we circumvented the formal design of a complete statechart diagram with at least 6937 states. The nine meta states are derived from the position and of the box and the objects contained therein.

5.5.1.3 Implementation

The implementation uses VRML97 as 3D modeling language. The main VRML file is `room.wrl`, located in the key experiment's dedicated folder `./1926_candle`. Most static and all interactive 3D assets are stored in the PROTO library file

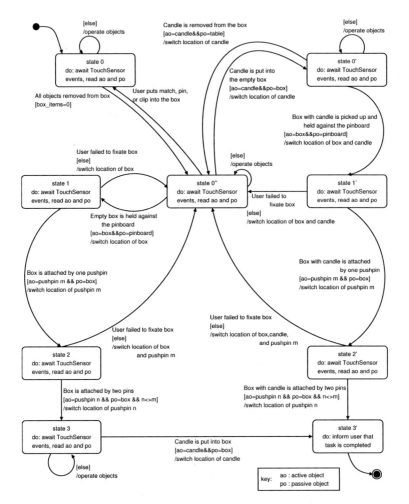

Figure 5.21: Duncker experiment (UML statechart diagram with nine super states)

Variable	Type	Description
box_state	Integer	Current state
box_items	Integer	Amount of objects (matches, pushpins, or paper clips) located in the box
active_object	String	Internal identifier of the active object
prev_active_object	String	Internal identifier of the preceding active object
selectmode	Boolean	Switch to determine whether or not the user can select a new active object
icon_active_object	Node	Icon to be displayed in the HUD

Table 5.5: Global variables used in Duncker experiment

ProtoDunckerObjects.wrl. Each interactive asset PROTO features parameters for its translation and rotation. The occurrence[12] of each interactive asset is controlled within individual Switch nodes that contain a sorted list of all required PROTO instances and use TouchSensor nodes for reading events (that is, a mouse click). At runtime, an object's predefined position is controlled by the Switch node parameter *whichChoice* that allows to switch between multiple PROTO representations. For example, *SwMatch1.whichChoice* is set from 1 to 0 if the object match #1 is put from the table into the box.

In the case of the candle object, this technique was extended to combine the object's location with its physical appearance. The Switch node *SwCandle* includes object representations that add a flickering flame to the candle's wick in order to visualize the lighting of the candle when "lit" with a match. The required visualization is achieved by setting the parameter *SwCandle.whichChoice* accordingly[13].

The visualization is initialized with a university room eqipped with the assets mentioned above. Figure 5.22 depicts the objects in their initial state, after the user has selected a pushpin. Figure 5.23 illustrates the object positions in the final state.

An implementation based on the UML statechart diagram described in Figure 5.21 requires additional global variables, such as the amount of objects located in the box and the current super state. The required global variables are described in Table 5.5.

For the implementation, the UML statechart diagram given in Figure 5.21 was further reduced. The amount of objects other than the candle that are located in the box is stored in the variable *box_items*. The location and condition of the candle is stored in *SwCandle.whichChoice*. Hence, the states 0, 0', and 0"

---

[12]Although the Switch node appears to visually "instantiate", "create", or "destroy" an object, there are no object-oriented methods involved in the code since VRML does not support them.

[13]A flame is visualized for *SwCandle.whichChoice* values of 4-6.

Figure 5.22: Duncker's candle problem: Screenshot (initial state, pushpin selected)

Figure 5.23: Duncker's candle problem: Screenshot (final state)

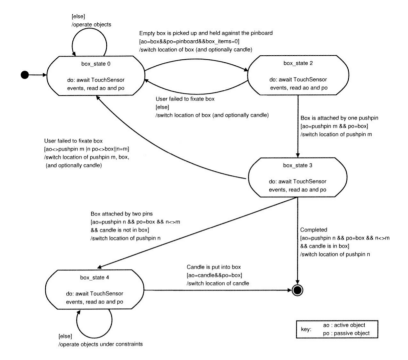

Figure 5.24: Duncker experiment (reduced UML statechart diagram with four super states)

can be merged. Furthermore, the sole difference between the state pairs (1, 1'), (2, 2'), and (3, 3') is the presence of the candle within the box. Hence, by using the values of *box_items* and *SwCandle.whichChoice*, the nine super states were reduced to four super states. The reduced statechart diagram with four super states, adapted guard conditions, and actions is shown in Figure 5.24.

The PROTO *bufferHUD* serves the following two purposes:

1. Buffer. It is used as a buffer that can be globally accessed by any Script node in *DirectOutput* mode and is used to store the global variables. This is required because VRML does not support global variables other than those stored as field values in nodes.

2. Visualization. The currently selected active object stored in the *active_object* variable is automatically visualized in the HUD. This is achieved by displaying an animated small-scaled PROTO instance of the selected interact-

ive 3D asset. The latter are predefined with the PROTO identifier prefix
"icon_".

The buffer's *prev_active_object* and *active_object* variables are needed for monitoring the correct execution order during the "attachment sequence". In this case,
the system has to analyze up to two previously used objects before changing its
super state.

Object interaction is controlled by object-related JavaScripts that are stored in
Script nodes. Every time the user selects an object, the system toggles the selection mode: if in selection mode, the user can select an active object. Otherwise,
the selected object is a passive object that is contextually used by the former
active object, as defined in Table 5.4. The currently selected object is displayed
in the HUD. If an undefined object combination is selected, the *prev_active_object*
and *active_object* variables are deleted and the selection mode is reset to active.

For each interactive object, a ROUTE is defined from the object's TouchSensor
touchTime event to the *touchTime* event of the corresponding Script node. Hence,
if clicked by the user, an object's JavaScript code block is executed: First, general conditions are checked, such as the analysis of the *prev_active_object* and
active_object variables for an ongoing "attachment sequence". If an ongoing "attachment sequence" is detected, the currently selected object is analyzed further.
If the latter is not operated in the correct order, the sequence is terminated and
all involved objects are reset. Otherwise, the sequence continues or, if passed
successfully, the system is set to super state 3.

Thereafter, the selection mode status is checked. In either case, actions are
executed accordingly, including the switching of the selection mode status, setting a new or empty icon in the HUD, or resetting the *active_object* variable to
an empty default value. In addition, required conditions are checked and actions are defined in this part of the code block. Any of the *box_state, box_items,
prev_active_object,* and *active_object* variables and the object's current position are
analyzed according to the conditions declared in the predefined object context,
the UML statechart diagram, and the aforementioned constraints and actions are
executed, which includes object repositioning, adapting global values, or a super
state transition. The conditions for the final state are checked in the ScrBox Script
node. Once the system has reached the final state a message is displayed using
the default HUD layout (see Section 4.5.7).

A complete exemplary Script node for pushpin #3 with comments is printed in
Listing 5.3.

5.5.2   Preceding/Succeeding experiments

Replicave does not feature any implementation of preceding or succeeding experiments in the context of Duncker's theory of functional fixedness.

Listing 5.3: Script node in Duncker experiment (Interaction with pushpin3 object)

```
DEF ScrPin3 Script  {
  eventIn SFTime touchTime
  field SFNode b USE Buffer
  field MFNode icon    icon_pin{}
  field MFNode noicon icon_empty{}
  field SFNode SwBox    USE SwBox
  field SFNode SwCandle USE SwCandle
  field SFNode SwPin3   USE SwPin3
  directOutput TRUE
  url ["javascript: function touchTime(value, time) {
    // if the user did not attach the box
    // and pin(s) correctly
    if (b.box_state==2&&b.prev_active_object=='pushpin3') {
    // box, candle, pin(s) fall back on the table
      SwBox.whichChoice = 0;
      if (SwPin3.whichChoice==3) SwPin3.whichChoice=1;
      if (SwCandle.whichChoice==3||SwCandle.whichChoice==6) {
        SwCandle.whichChoice=0; }
      // reset state
      b.box_state = 0;
      //reset active object and HUD
      b.active_object = '';
      b.icon_active_object = noicon;
      //switch select mode
      b.selectmode = TRUE;
      return;
    }
    if (b.selectmode) {
      b.active_object = 'pushpin3';
      b.icon_active_object = icon;
      b.selectmode = FALSE;
    }
    else {
      b.prev_active_object = b.active_object;
      b.active_object = '';
      b.icon_active_object = noicon;
      b.selectmode = TRUE;
    }
  }"]
}
```

5.5.3   Conclusion

A 3D reconstruction of Duncker's historical candle problem was presented, based on geometric and discrete modeling. The implementation represents a feasible solution with regard to contemporary consumer market hardware and interfaces and web-based 3D modeling languages (that is, VRML), as required by the Replicave project's specifications.

Future extended implementations, based on the described geometric and discrete interaction models, may include support for native 3D I/O devices (for example, 3D gloves, haptic devices, 3D visual devices) that increase the user's sensual experience. A 3D motion tracker may monitor the exact 3D movement of objects and may allow the visualization of continuous object movements, by which the requirement of predefined discrete object positions could be overcome. Assuming that the FSM model is slightly changed by mapping states to (non-overlapping) 3D regions (i.e.: 3D clouds), instead of discrete coordinates, the existing FSM model could be used further.

Chapter 6

Evaluation

The implementation of the Replicave framework system was evaluated with a focus on usability of the framework system and 3D assets that were developed during a study project during the summer semester 2006. In particular, the survey focused on the following aspects:

- 2D vs. 3D design

- Conceptual design

- User interface (visual design, browser-specific controls and additional hardware interfaces, system-specific HUD icons, spatial layout, avatar design, and interaction)

An online questionnaire survey was used as the main research method.

6.1 Questionnaire survey

Eleven persons participated in the anonymous and voluntary survey. The questionnaire consists of a person-related section and five sections covering the topics listed above. The survey was developed with the survey and questionnaire authoring software PHP Surveyor[1]. Survey-specific data is stored in the database[2] phpsurveyor. A printed version of the questionnaire is given in Appendix A.6.

All participants had at least basic computer knowledge, two of which had also basic knowledge about psychology, including the only female participant. Nine participants were aged 20-29, two belonged to the age group 30-39.

The survey results are given in the following section.

---

[1] http://www.phpsurveyor.org/ [Accessed 17 June 2006]

[2] Due to reserved table names, the survey tool should use a separate MySQL database. For convenience, the phpsurveyor database is stored on the same server as the VirtLab database.

6.2 Key findings

6.2.1 2D vs. 3D

Ten out of the eleven participants (90.91%) agreed that a 3D presentation of the experiments generally appeared more realistic to them than a 2D presentation. In particular, all participants (100%) agreed that the representation of a virtual 3D rat in the Skinner box appeared more realistic than the 2D-based version given on the project's 2D web site [Wor04].

Another question addressed the potential impact of integrating 2D experiments into a 3D framework system. With regard to the 2D Skinner experiments [Wor04], the participants were asked how they would consider preceding/succeeding 2D experiments as compared to 3D ones. Here, potential media discontinuities in content visualization were not considered to adversely affect the system's concept. Only two respondents agreed that adding 2D experiments could cause content inconsistency. All participants agreed that 2D experiments are important additional knowledge sources (see Table 6.1).

How would you consider preceding/succeeding 2D experiments as compared to 3D ones?	Number of responses
They are important additional knowledge sources.	11
A well-designed alternation of 2D and 3D might offer advantages.	6
They might offer a certain relieving variation.	2
They could cause a content inconsistency.	2
They don't fit into the concept due to the switch between 2D and 3D content.	0
They could appear out of the context.	0

Table 6.1: 2D vs. 3D laboratory

On the question "Are the experiments easier to comprehend through a 3D-based representation, as compared to a 2D-based representation?", 90.91% said that the experiments were easier to comprehend in 3D, 9.09% claimed that there was no difference between a 2D and a 3D representation, and none of the participants agreed that comprehension was more difficult in the 3D-based implementation (see Table 6.2).

Are the experiments easier to comprehend through a 3D-based representation, as compared to a 2D-based representation?	Percentage
Easier to comprehend in 3D	90.91%
No difference between 2D and 3D	9.09%
More difficult to comprehend in 3D	0%

Table 6.2: Demand for additional multimedia hardware input interfaces

These results confirm an advanced degree of realism through the application of the synthesis model described in Section 3.3 and a 3D visualization. Although more than 90% of the participants stated that they believed they could comprehend the experiments better through a 3D visualization, this does not allow us to draw conclusions about the pedagogical impact of the Replicave system. However, we interpret these results as a motivation for further pedagogical research.

6.2.2 Conceptual design

A vital element in the conceptual design is the integration of preceding and succeeding experiments. All participants (100%) agreed that their understanding of the historical experiment improved through the integration of preceding and succeeding experiments and that this integration was generally desirable for the representation of the complete historical context of a psychological theory, regardless of a 2D or 3D implementation. A majority of participants (81.82%) stated that knowledge of the historical experiment would improve the understanding of preceding and succeeding experiments.

6.2.3 User interface

6.2.3.1 3D visual design

The framework system and the psychological laboratories were rated with regard to the overall visual 3D design. On a scale from 1-4 (very good - bad), the visual design of the framework system (entrance hall, media rooms, gallery, elevator, floors without laboratories) was rated with an average of 1.45.

The 3D representation of the psychological laboratories was described as "entertaining and instructive" by more than half of the participants (54.55%), as "inspiring and instructive" by another 27.27%, whereas 18.18% stated it was "entertaining, but not instructive".

6.2.3.2   Browser-specific controls

The usability of the VRML browser's navigational controls with default hardware interfaces (that is, mouse and keyboard) were rated on a scale from 1-4 (1-intuitive, 4-complicated) with regard to navigation within the VRML environment. Results showed that the participants rated the mouse (2.36) as slightly better suited for navigation than the keyboard (2.45).

Almost half of the participants (45.45%) miss a beam-to navigation, that is, an automatic translocation of the user's avatar to a ground-based location selected by a mouse-click within the 3D world. At the time of the evaluation, the "beam-to navigation" feature had just been integrated into the VRML plugin. Since the latest versions of the VRML plugin can be configured to use beam-to navigation in any VRML environment, the demands for this navigation method can be met.

The reasons for these results are uncertain and might be caused by a low degree of familiarization with the browser interface, as some user-specific parameters that influence the interaction behavior of the interfaces can be individually configured in the VRML browser (for example, speed, beam-to navigation).

A more detailed investigation of these issues requires quantification of the participant's individual skill in operating the VRML browser and should therefore be conducted in a special usability lab.

6.2.3.3   Additional hardware input interfaces

Despite the use of a concept keyboard in the Ebbinghaus experiment, mouse and keyboard are the common hardware input interfaces. The participants were asked to select which hardware input interface they would like to use additionally (see Table 6.3). The most frequently selected interface was speech control (7 responses), followed by 3D glove (6), Joystick (4), Concept keyboard (4), 3D mouse (3), gamepad (2), and mobile devices (2). The cause for the strong interest in speech control could not be determined. However, speech input should be coupled with speech output, which would imply speech-based extensions of many interactive objects.

Like the concept keyboard, the 3D glove is a cost-extensive device which could most likely not be afforded by the majority of potential users. Joysticks and gamepads are alternative and affordable input devices in navigating, which might be integrated in future versions.

Interface	Number of responses
Speech control	▨▨▨▨ 7
3D glove	▨▨▨ 6
Joystick	▨▨ 4
Concept Keyboard	▨▨ 4
3D mouse	▨ 3
Gamepad	▨ 2
Mobile device	▨ 2

Table 6.3: Demand for additional multimedia hardware input interfaces

6.2.3.4 System-specific HUD icons

The default HUD icons of the framework system are used for displaying interactive, animated 3D buttons for an information panel, a graphical timeline image, and an exit shortcut (see Section 4.5.7 and Figures 4.5, 4.6, and 4.7). The HUD icons were mainly rated as intuitive or very intuitive (see Table 6.4). Experiment-specific HUD icons have not been evaluated.

The HUD icons are...	Percentage
Very intuitive	▨▨ 36.36%
Intuitive	▨▨▨▨ 63.64%
Satisfactory	0
Less intuitive	0
Rather irritating	0

Table 6.4: HUD icons rating (framework system)

6.2.3.5 Spatial layout

Spatial layout is crucial to the user's ability to navigate through the system. Participants were asked to select those areas, to which they could easily find their way from (a) the entrance hall and (b) the floor.

The large media room and the gallery could most easily be found from the entrance hall (81.82%), followed by the elevator (63.64%), and the laboratories (45.45%), the latter being the only non-adjacent area to the entrance hall. From the floors (that is, from the conceptional metaphor or vertical connector) the laboratories could be found most easily (100%), followed by the elevator (90.91%) and small media room (72.73%). Again, the non-adjacent areas entrance hall (54.55%), large media room (36.36%), and gallery (9.09%) received lower ratings.

Finally, the participants were asked about their opinion on the building metaphor
with regard to easy navigation. A majority of participants (81.82%) stated that
they liked the layout "the way it is", another group (18.18%) claimed that the
walls were acceptable, but that they considered the design to be too conventional.
The walls were not criticized as being too restrictive or complex in navigation (see
Table 6.5).

How do you consider navigating through floors and rooms?	Percentage
I like it the way it is.	81.82%
The walls are acceptable, but the design is too conventional.	18.18%
The walls are too restrictive.	0%
Complex (Loss of orientation possible).	0%

Table 6.5: Navigation through building metaphor

With regard to the idea of a "museum without walls" [Mal56], the participants
were asked how they would consider the idea of placing all laboratories into a
single open environment without walls or doors. Despite the hypothetical nature
of this question, only one participant (9.09%) favored a layout without walls
and doors. An equal number of responses expresses no clear preference, and the
majority (81.82%) stated that they prefer the existing layout (see Table 6.6).

How do you consider the idea of placing all laboratories into a single open environment without walls or doors?	Percentage
I prefer the present layout with doors and walls.	81.82%
I think both layouts would have their share of advantages and disadvantages.	9.09%
I would prefer a layout without walls and doors.	9.09%

Table 6.6: "Open environment" vs. building metaphor

Participants were also asked how quickly they could acquire a spatial orientation
in the system. It turned out that a majority could quickly (54.55%) or even very
quickly (36.36%) find their way through the system (see Table 6.7).

How quickly did you find your way through the system?	Percentage
Quickly	54.55%
Very quickly	36.36%
Slowly	9.09%

Table 6.7: Spatial orientation

Summarizing, the existing spatial layout allows users to easily navigate through the system and the metaphorical design (building metaphor) is also accepted by the majority of participants.

6.2.3.6 Avatar design

The question focused in this section is to what extend the VRML-based static avatars optimized for web-based transmission (that is, with a relatively low number of polygons) could remedy the potential issue of a low degree of perceived agency by the user (see Section 4.5.6) with regard to the avatar's visual and interaction design.

Although a majority of participants rated the avatars' visual design as "authentic" (90.91%) and "almost authentic"(9.09%, see Table 6.8), nearly half of the participants (45.46%) described the perceived ambiance as unrealistic, 27.27% as natural, and 27.27% as "alive" (see Table 6.9).

With regard to avatar functionality, 90.91% agreed that the functionality offered by the "visitor" avatars was sufficient, whereas 81.82% found the same to be true for the "guard" model. Additional avatar-related interaction was demanded for the functionalities "providing information about the framework system" (number of responses: 6), "giving an introduction into the system" (5), and "reception desk" (4). A guided tour and more general feedback was only demanded two times (see Table 6.10).

The graphical avatar representation is...	Percentage
Authentic	90.91%
Almost authentic	9.09%
Slightly authentic	0%
Not authentic	0%

Table 6.8: Authenticity of avatar design

The avatars in the public places let me perceive an ambiance that is...	Percentage
Alive	▬ 27.27%
Natural	▬ 27.27%
Unrealistic	▬▬ 45.46%
Irritating	0%

Table 6.9: Perceived agency with regard to avatars in framework system

Where would you expect more interaction with avatars?	Number of responses
Information about framework system	▬▬▬ 6
Introduction into the system	▬▬ 5
Reception desk	▬▬ 4
Guided Tour	▬ 2
Feedback	▬ 2
Other	0

Table 6.10: Demand for more interaction with avatars

Hence, the avatars have an authentic visual design and provide a sufficient degree of functionality, although an environment that is perceived as more "natural" and "realistic" would require the design and implementation of additional interactive avatar features.

6.2.3.7 Interaction

Single interactive elements within the framework system include the media assets, film projector, gallery information boards, logon terminal, elevator, content explorer, and doors. Due to their specific character and since they are not omnipresent (as compared, for example, to interactive control or navigation buttons on a 2D GUI, like a web browser) these have not been evaluated because a usability test in a controlled environment, like a usability lab, would most likely deliver more exact, that is, comparable, results than by means of a questionnaire survey.

However, the results concerning navigation through the spatial layout (see Section 6.2.3.5) imply at least a sufficient degree of interaction of the elevator control panel and the laboratory doors for navigational needs.

In a final question, participants expressed additional interaction demands for the small media room (Number of responses: 2), gallery and laboratories (each: 3), and for the large media room and entrance area (each: 4), which implies that the majority of participants was satisfied with the overall degree of interaction in the various areas of the framework system.

Chapter 7

Conclusion

7.1 Summary

There are only few publications and implementations concerned with synthesizing historical psychological experiments in virtual environments. This thesis primarily presents a theoretical approach (modeling pipeline) for the synthesis of replicated (historical and non-historical) virtual scientific laboratories that allow the conduction of *interactive* and *reversible* psychological experiments based on deterministic or non-deterministic *simulation models*.

The discussion of metaphorical design considerations have resulted in a theoretical approach for the design of parameterizable conceptional and temporal metaphors that allow the structured spatial and temporal arrangement of content created by the application of the synthesis model. The implementation of template-based temporal metaphors underline the extensibility of the concept.

Another result is the extension of an existing structural model for a virtual museum into a structural model for a virtual environment for replicated experiments, which is not limited to psychology-related content. This structural model supports the implementation process by defining special services that can be mapped to software modules (for example, database, web server) within a (software) system architecture.

The application of the aforementioned theoretical approaches result in the implementation of the Replicave system and prove the feasibility of the concept. A wide range of aspects has been covered: deterministic and non-deterministic simulation models, special hardware interfaces, integration of existing 2D/3D content, experiments, in which the user takes different roles (researcher, test animal), and the integration of a database for the recording of data sets.

The system is a web-based virtual 3D museum environment that consists of a modular framework system and various replicated laboratories. With regard to its educational purpose the system represents a constructivist learning environment in the domain of psychology. From a museum-related perspective, it represents a virtual museum that contributes to the preservation of digital heritage.

The evaluation has shown that users prefer 3D-based visualization for the Skinner experiment. On the other hand, the implementation of the Skinner experiments has demonstrated that the production of 3D content and complex simulation models is expensive and should be thoroughly considered. The integration of static avatars into a virtual museum framework environment has revealed the feasibility of adding social ambiance to a virtual environment at a relatively low cost. The classical design of the building metaphor used, was rated positively by the users. As was the implementation of the metaphorical design with regard to navigation.

7.2 Discussion and further research

The presented work describes theoretical approaches and required technical efforts for the replication of classical psychological experiments in virtual environments. Due to its modular and dynamic content base, the Replicave system is open to future modification and extensions. Hence, it can be regarded as a complex proof of concept rather than as a static and finished product. As already mentioned in the text, the system could be further enhanced. Several potential aspects of further research can be identified.

First, other non-deterministic simulation models for modeling animal behavior could be scrutinized that allow a better trade-off between model complexity, model control, and performance. Although the presented model based on Markov chains represents a working solution, a model refinement would increase its present degree of complexity, which would most likely result in performance issues. Other techniques used in the field of artificial intelligence and artificial learning might offer a more flexible approach.

Another important aspect crucial to the success of virtual 3D systems is the social space property. As shown in the evaluation, a relatively large percentage of users had a low degree of personal agency, despite the "realistic" graphical design of the avatars. Two methods to remedy this issue are the creation of a multi-user virtual environment and the development of more interactive or animated avatars.

The system could be further evaluated. Experts from the educational sciences could scrutinize the pedagogical aspects of the system. In addition, other hardware-specific usability issues could be further investigated in a special usability lab.

The system could be equipped with a more user-friendly database query and information visualization tool for discussing measured data records in single-user and classroom scenarios.

Finally an overall extension of the framework system could be considered. This may include the integration and evaluation of additional 3D hardware and an extension of the template-based approach through additional metaphorical design patterns, which might lead to a fully customizable 3D framework environment, dynamically generated based on visual, metaphorical, language, and hardware specific user preferences.

Appendix A

Appendix

A.1 Development software

Task	Software product(s)
3D modelling (VRML)	Virtock Technologies Spazz3D
3D modeling	Maxon Cinema 4D XL 7, Blender
VRML text editor	Parallelgraphics VRML Pad
2D graphics tool	Adobe Photoshop, The GIMP
Text processing	MS Word, OpenOffice
PHP text editor	IDM UltraEdit-32
Web browser	MS Internet Explorer
VRML browser	BS Contact
Java IDE	Eclipse
Database administration interface	phpMyAdmin
Database	MySQL
Remote server administration	SSH

Table A.1: Development software listed by tasks

A.2   Session variables (Overview)

A.2.1   hc_root

The hc_root variable is used to store the selected historical present.

Value	Description
now	Default historical present
¿folder name¿	Any folder name from the ./labs directory containing all experiments and multimedia files on a psychologist that is also listed in the $psychos_allowed array in ./labs/main.conf.inc.php.

Table A.2: Values of hc_root

A.2.2   hc_position

The hc_position variable is used to store a meta description of the initial viewpoint in a selected historical present.

Value	Description (position)	Description (viewing direction)
-1	"In the elevator"	"out of the elevator toward the floor"
0	"In the floor in front of the small media room's door"	"toward the center of the floor"
$n = 1..6$	"In the floor in front of the door leading to the n-th experiment"	"toward the center of the floor"

Table A.3: Values of hc_position

A.2.3 vc_position

The vc_position variable is used to store the meta state of the selected historical present.

Value	Description
0	Default historical present selected (hc_root='now')
1	otherwise

Table A.4: Values of vc_position

A.3 Auxiliary functions (framework system)

Function name	Description
printfile($fn)	Prints file $fn linewise to standard output. (Used to integrate statically stored non-compressed VRML code.)
template_printfile($fn)	Prints file $fn, which must be located in a template subfolder, linewise to standard output.
parsedir($dirs)	Parses files in a comma-separated list of directories ($dirs) for supported multimedia file type extensions and returns a list of multimedia file URNs ordered by video, text, and image data. (Used to generate shelf content in media rooms.)
parseimagedir($dir)	Parses files in a single directory ($dir) for supported image file extensions and returns a list of image file URNs. (Used to generate dynamic picture frames in horizontal connector.)
array_alternate_multisort()	Sort a multi-dimensional PHP array.

Table A.5: PHP functions in ./framework/auxfunctions.inc.php

A.4   Files and directories in the `/replicave/labs` folder and subfolders

File/*Folder*	Task	Parsed by...
`main.conf.inc.php`	Definition of psychologist-related folder name(s) containing content approved for publication.	`contentlist.wrl.php`
psychologist	Folder containing all experiments and multimedia files on one psychologist.	
`loc_de.inc.php/` `loc_en.inc.php`	Localization files containing meta data.	`contentlist.wrl.php,` `hconnector.php`
`psy.conf.inc.php`	Definition of folder name(s) containing experiments approved for publication.	`hconnector.php`
lab	Folder containing all files on a selected experiment	
`index.php`	Initial file for launching a selected experiment. Contains either a single 3D experiment or contains a selection algorithm that forwards the user to a dedicated subfolder.	Linked by `hconnector.php`

Table A.6: Files and directories in the `/replicave/labs` folder and subfolders

A.5 Function **create_thresholds** in default template

Listing A.1: Threshold creation in default template

```
function  create_thresholds($hc_root ,  $data ,  $lang)  {
    // Define auxiliary function
...  // print_threshold($pos ,$active ,$type ,$lab)
    // for VRML code output
    $t  =  min(count($data) ,  6);      // Thresholds limit
    if($t>1)  {  // If more than one experiment
        print_threshold (0 ,1 ,1 ,0);
        for( $i =1;$i<$t +1;$i++)  {
            print_threshold ($i ,1 ,0 ,$i );  }
        for( $i=$t +1;$i <7;$i++)  {
            print_threshold ($i ,0 ,0 ,$i );  }
    }  else  {  // Only one experiment
        print_threshold (0 ,0 ,0 ,0);
        print_threshold (1 ,1 ,1 ,0);
        print_threshold (2 ,1 ,0 ,1);
        for( $i =3;$i <7;$i++)  {
            print_threshold ($i ,0 ,0 ,0);  }
    }
    include("vconnector.php");    // Print vconnector threshold
    return ;
}
```

Listing A.2: Auxiliary function for VRML code output

```
function print_threshold($pos,$active,$type,$lab){
    //pos: Position 0-6, active: Door(1) or Wall(0),
    //type: Media room(1) - other (0)
    global $data, $psyname, $hc_root;
    $translation=array('0 0 -28.5','-6.7 0 -25','6.7 0 -25', \
             '14 0 -15.5','14 0 -7.5','-14 0 -15.5','-14 0 -7.5');
    $rotation   =array('0 1 0 0','0 1 0 0.86','0 1 0 -0.86', \
             '0 1 0 0','0 1 0 3.1416','0 1 0 0','0 1 0 3.1416');
    $options    = "hc_position=$pos";
    $text1 = word_wrap($psyname,12);
    switch($type) {
      case 1:
        $text2 = tl("t_mediaroom");
        $url   = "mroom_s.wrl.php?$options"; break;
      default:
        $text2 = word_wrap($data[$lab-1]['tl_section'].' \
                   ('.$data[$lab-1]['tl_year'].')',23);
        $url   = $data[$lab-1]['path']."index.php?$options";
    }
    switch($active) {
      case 1:
        $vrml_proto = "WallWithDoor";
        $infoparms  = "text1 \"$text1\"
                    text2 \"$text2\"
                    url \"$url\""; break;
      default:
        $vrml_proto = "Wall2";
        $infoparms  = '';    // No parameters required
    }
    if ($pos < 0) { ... }    // Error handling
    else {
      echo"DEF T$pos $vrml_proto {
              translation     $translation[$pos]
              rotation        $rotation[$pos]
              $infoparms }";
    }
}
```

A.6 Questionnaire

Interaktive Benutzerbefragung (Replicave)

A

A_Age: Welcher Altersgruppe gehören Sie an?
Bitte wählen Sie nur **eine Antwort** aus:
- ☐ 0-19
- ☐ 20-29
- ☐ 30-39
- ☐ 40-64
- ☐ 65 oder älter

B_Gender: Bitte nennen Sie Ihr Geschlecht:
Bitte wählen Sie nur **eine Antwort** aus:
- ☐ Weiblich
- ☐ Männlich

C_AffinityComputer: Besitzen Sie Grundkenntnisse im Umgang mit PCs?
Bitte wählen Sie nur **eine Antwort** aus:
- ☐ Ja
- ☐ Nein

D_psychologie: Besitzen Sie Vorkenntnisse im Bereich Psychologie?
Bitte wählen Sie nur **eine Antwort** aus:
- ☐ Ja
- ☐ Nein

B

1: Halten Sie die graphische Darstellung der Avatare für authentisch?
Bitte wählen Sie nur **eine Antwort** aus:
- ☐ Authentisch
- ☐ Fast authentisch
- ☐ Wenig authentisch
- ☐ Nicht authentisch

2: In den öffentlichen Bereichen empfinde ich die Atmosphäre durch die Anwesenheit der Avatare als:
Bitte wählen Sie nur **eine Antwort** aus:
- ☐ Belebt
- ☐ Natürlich
- ☐ Unwirklich, wie im Wachsfigurenkabinett
- ☐ Irritierend

3: Halten Sie die von den Avataren in Form von Museumsbesuchern vorgehaltenen Funktionen für hinreichend?
Bitte wählen Sie nur **eine Antwort** aus:
- ☐ Ja
- ☐ Nein

4: Halten Sie die von den Avataren in Form von Angestellten/Wärtern vorgehaltenen Funktionen für hinreichend?
Bitte wählen Sie nur **eine Antwort** aus:
- ☐ Ja
- ☐ Nein

5: Vermissen Sie Interaktion mit den Avataren? Falls ja, in welchem der aufgeführten Bereiche?

<u>Wählen Sie **alle** zutreffenden Antworten</u>
- Auskunft zum Rahmensystem
- Guided Tour
- Einführung in das System
- Anmeldung bzw. Reception
- Feedback
- Sonstiges

C

1: Erweitern die vorhandenen Extensionen bzw. Vor-/Nachläuferexperimente Ihr Verständnis der historischen Experimente?

<u>Bitte wählen Sie nur **eine Antwort** aus:</u>
- Ja
- Nein

2: Ist Ihrer Meinung nach zum besseren Verständnis der Extension bzw. des Vor-/Nachläuferexperimentes eine Kenntnis des jeweiligen Schlüsselexperiments notwendig?

<u>Bitte wählen Sie nur **eine Antwort** aus:</u>
- Ja
- Nein

3: Sind Ihrer Meinung nach Extensionen bzw. Vor-/Nachläuferexperimente grundsätzlich wünschenwert zur Vermittlung des kompletten historischen Kontextes einer psychologischen Theorie?

<u>Bitte wählen Sie nur **eine Antwort** aus:</u>
- Ja
- Nein

4: Oft bietet sich aus Kostengründen die Darstellung von 2D-Experimenten an. Wie beurteilen Sie die Extensionen bzw. Vor-/Nachläuferexperimente, die nur zwei-dimensional (2D) implementiert sind im Vergleich zu drei-dimensionalen (3D) Laboren?

<u>Wählen Sie **alle** zutreffenden Antworten</u>
- Sie sind als zusätliche Wissensquelle wichtig.
- Sie passen wegen des Sprungs von 3D nach 2D nicht ins Konzept.
- Sie könnten aus dem Zusammenhang gerissen wirken.
- Sie könnten sich als störend auf die Konsistenz von Inhalt und Darstellung auswirken.
- Sie könnten eine gewisse Abwechslung bieten.
- Bei richtiger Gestaltung könnte ein Rhythmus von 2D und 3D Vorteile aufweisen.

D

1: Wie empfinden Sie die Navigation in der VRML-Umgebung mit Hilfe der Maus?

<u>Bitte wählen Sie nur **eine Antwort** aus:</u>
- Intuitiv
- Leicht
- Gewöhnungsbedürftig
- Kompliziert

2: Wie beurteilen Sie die Navigation in der VRML-Umgebung mit Hilfe der Tastatur?

<u>Bitte wählen Sie nur **eine Antwort** aus:</u>
- Intuitiv
- Leicht
- Gewöhnungsbedürftig
- Kompliziert

3: Wie beurteilen Sie die Darstellung der 3D-Icons im Heads-Up-Display (HUD) auf deren Bedeutung hin?

Bitte wählen Sie nur **eine Antwort** aus:

- Sehr intuitiv
- Intuitiv
- Zufriedenstellend
- Wenig intuitiv
- Eher irritierend

4: In welchem Bereich/welchen Bereichen wünschen Sie sich mehr Interaktivität?

Wählen Sie **alle** zutreffenden Antworten

- Galerie
- Laborräume
- Großer Medienraum (Erdgeschoss)
- Kleiner Medienraum (in den Laboretagen)
- Eingangsbereich

5: Welche multimedialen Eingabenschnittstellen würden Sie sich zusätzlich wünschen?

Wählen Sie **alle** zutreffenden Antworten

- Gamepad
- Joystick
- Spracheingabe
- 3D-Handschuh
- 3D-Maus
- Mobiles Gerät
- Concept Keyboard

E

1: Wie beurteilen Sie die gestalterische Qualität der 3D-Darstellung im Rahmensystem (Empfangshalle, Medienräume, Galerie, Aufzug, Flure ohne Laborräume)?

Bitte wählen Sie nur **eine Antwort** aus:

- Sehr gut gelungen
- Gut gelungen
- Akzeptabel
- Nicht gelungen

2: Wie beurteilen Sie die 3D-Darstellung in den psychologischen Laboren?

Bitte wählen Sie nur **eine Antwort** aus:

- Inspirierend und lehrreich
- Unterhaltend und lehrreich
- Unterhaltend, aber nicht lehrreich
- Langweilig und nicht lehrreich

3: Wirkt für Sie die Darstellung der Experimente durch Verwendung von 3D generell realistischer, anstelle einer 2D-Darstellung?

Bitte wählen Sie nur **eine Antwort** aus:

- Ja
- Nein

3b: Wirkt für Sie die Darstellung der Ratte in einer Skinnerbox durch Verwendung von 3D realistischer im Vergleich zu einer 2D-Darstellung, wie sie unter http://schluesselexp.uni-duisburg.de/tutorium/skinner/szene_3/index.htm (neues Fenster) gegeben wird?

Bitte wählen Sie nur **eine Antwort** aus:

⌐ Ja

⌐ Nein

4: Sind die thematisierten Experimente durch die 3D-Darstellung generell leichter nachzuvollziehen als durch eine 2D-Darstellung?

Bitte wählen Sie nur **eine Antwort** aus:

⌐ Leichter nachzuvollziehen in 3D

⌐ Es besteht kein Unterschied zwischen 2D und 3D

⌐ Schwerer nachzuvollziehen in 3D

F

1: Von der Eingangshalle aus ist der Weg zu folgenden Bereichen leicht zu finden:

Wählen Sie **alle** zutreffenden Antworten

⌐ Zu den Laborräumen

⌐ Zum großen Medienraum

⌐ Zum Aufzug

⌐ Zur Galerie

⌐ Zur Empfangshalle

2: Von den Fluren aus ist der Weg zu folgenden Bereichen leicht zu finden:

Wählen Sie **alle** zutreffenden Antworten

⌐ Zu den Laborräumen

⌐ Zum kleinen Medienraum

⌐ Zum großen Medienraum

⌐ Zur Galerie

⌐ Zur Empfangshalle

⌐ Zum Aufzug

3: Vermissen Sie eine Click-To / Beam-To-Navigation im System?

Bitte wählen Sie nur **eine Antwort** aus:

⌐ Ja

⌐ Nein

4: Wie beurteilen Sie die Navigation durch Flure und Räume?

Bitte wählen Sie nur **eine Antwort** aus:

⌐ Die Wände sind mir zu restriktiv

⌐ Die Wände sind akzeptabel, aber das Design ist mir zu konventionell

⌐ Unübersichtlich (Orientierungsverlust möglich)

⌐ Es gefällt mir so, wie es ist

5: Wie beurteilen Sie die Überlegung, sämtliche Labore in einer einzigen komplett offenen Umgebung ohne Wände oder Türen zu platzieren?

Bitte wählen Sie nur **eine Antwort** aus:

⌐ Ein Layout ohne Wände und Türen fände ich besser

⌐ Ich finde, dass beide Layouts gleichermaßen Vor- und Nachteile besitzen

⌐ Ich bevorzuge das aktuelle Layout mit Türen und Wänden

6: Haben Sie sich schnell im System zurechtgefunden?

Bitte wählen Sie nur **eine Antwort** aus:

⌐ Nur langsam zurechtgefunden

⌐ Ziemlich schnell zurechtgefunden

⌐ Schnell zurechtgefunden

⌐ Kaum zurechtgefunden

⌐ Überhaupt nicht zurechtgefunden

List of Figures

List of Tables

Listings

Bibliography

[ADSW00] L. Alvarez, R. Deriche, J. Sanchez, and J. Weickert. Dense disparity map estimation respecting image discontinuities: a PDE and scalespace based approach, 2000.

[AF98] N. Ashdown and S. Forestiero. *A Guide to VRML 2.0 and an Evaluation of VRML Modelling Tools*, 1998. Retrieved March 11, 2004, from http://www.agocg.ac.uk/train/vrml2rep/cover.htm.

[AGK94] T. Alloway, J. Graham, and L. Krames. Sniffy, the virtual rat: Simulated operant conditioning. Behavior research methods. *Instruments and Computers*, 26(2):134–141, 1994.

[Ang79] W.F. Angermeier. *Psychologie des Lernens*. Film, Universität Erlangen-Nürnberg, FIM Psychologie, 1979.

[ASRN01] B. Asmuss, A. Scriba, J. Reiche, and L. Nentwig. The LeMO Project - Development of an internet multimedia information system of 20th century German history: Aims and results. *ICHIM 2001, Milan, Italy*, 1:307–322, 2001.

[BBHW02] C. Blais, D. Brutzman, J. Harney, and J. Weekley. Web-based 3D reconstruction of scenarios for limited objective experiments. 2002. Retrieved March 11, 2004, from http://www.movesinstitute.org/Publications/S192_Blais.pdf.

[BC97a] G. Bell and R. Carey. *The Annotated VRML 2.0 Reference Manual*. Addison-Wesley, 1997.

[BC97b] H.A. Bridges and D. Charitos. On architectural design in virtual environments. *Design Studies*, 18(2):143–154, April 1997.

[BGMS01] C. Braun, M. Gründl, C. Marberger, and C. Scherber. *Beautycheck - Ursachen und Folgen von Attraktivität. Projektabschlussbericht.*, 2001. Retrieved February 14, 2006, from http://www.uni-regensburg.de/Fakultaeten/phil_Fak_II/Psychologie/Psy_II/beautycheck/bericht/beauty_ho_zensiert.pdf.

173

[Bjo93]   D.W. Bjork. *B.F. Skinner - A life.* BasicBooks, 1993.

[BL00]   N. Buderham and H. Lifshitz. Open field behavior in a rat: A computer simulation. Technical report, University of Jerusalem, Israel, 2000. Retrieved March 11, 2004, from alice.nc.huji.ac.il/ ~yaelniv/PsychSeminar/NaphtaliHanan.doc.

[BL02]   N. Baloian and W. Luther. Visualization for the mind's eye. In Stephan Diehl, editor, *Software Visualization, State-of-the-Art Survey LNCS 2269*, pages 354–367. Springer, 2002.

[BLM+03a]   D. Biella, W. Luther, G. Mietzel, H.-P. Musahl, and L. Wormuth. Replication of Classical Psychological Experiments in Virtual Environments (Replicave). In *Proceedings of the 2nd European Conference on eLearning (ECEL2003)*, pages 81 – 91, 2003.

[BLM+03b]   D. Biella, W. Luther, G. Mietzel, H.-P. Musahl, and L. Wormuth. Replication of classical psychological experiments in virtual laboratories in a historical context. In A. Méndez-Vilas, J.A. Mesa González, and J. Mesa González, editors, *Advances in Technology-based Education: Toward a Knowledge-based Society, Vol. 3*, pages 1785–1789, 2003.

[BZ03]   F. Bick and K. Zeppenfeld. Zur Reliabilität und Validität von Online-Experimenten. Multimediale Replikation eines Gedächnispsychologischen Experiments (Sperling, 1960) als Lerneinheit für die Weiterbildung. Master's thesis, University of Duisburg-Essen, 2003.

[Cer99]   C. Cerulli. Exploiting the potential of 3D navigable virtual exhibition spaces. *Museums and the Web 1999*, 1999. Retrieved March 11, 2004, from http://www.archimuse.com/mw99/papers/ cerulli/cerulli.html.

[Che95]   S. E. Chen. Quicktime VR - An Image-based Approach to Virtual Environment Navigation. In *Proceedings of the ACM SIGGRAPH 95 Conference*, pages 29–38, 1995.

[DBB+04]   S. Dietz, H. Besser, A. Borda, K. Geber, and P. Lévy. Virtual Museum (of Canada): The Next Generation, October 2004.

[Der01]   H. Dersch. *Panorama Tools*, 2001. Retrieved March 11, 2004, from http://www.path.unimelb.edu.au/~dersch/.

[DFAB04]   A. Dix, J. Finlay, G.G. Abowd, and R. Beale. *Human computer interaction.* Prentice Hall, 3rd edition, 2004.

[Dic99]   M. Dickey. *3D Virtual Worlds and Learning: An Analysis of the Impact of Design Affordances and Limitations in Active Worlds, blaxxun interactive, and OnLive! Traveler; and A Study of the Implementation of Active Worlds for Formal and Informal Education.* PhD thesis, Ohio State University, 1999. Retrieved March 11, 2004, from http://michele.netlogix.net/side3/dissertation.htm.

[Die97]   S. Diehl. VRML++: A Language for Object-Oriented Virtual-Reality Models. In *Proceedings of the 24th International Conference on Technology of Object-Oriented Languages and Systems (TOOLS97), Beijing, China,* 1997.

[Die98]   S. Diehl. Object-Oriented Animations with VRML++. In *Proceedings of the Virtual Environments Conference and 4th Eurographics Workshop, Stuttgart, Germany,* 1998.

[Dil00]   P. Dillenbourg. Virtual Learning Environments. *EUN Conference 2000, Learning in the New Millennium: Building new Education Strategies for Schools,* Workshop on Virtual Environments, 2000.

[Dun26]   K. Duncker. A qualitative (experimental and theoretical) study of productive thinking (solving of comprehensible problems). *Pedagogical Seminary,* (33):642–708, 1926.

[Dun45]   K. Duncker. On problem solving. *Psychological Monographs,* 58(5), 1945.

[Ebb85]   H. Ebbinghaus. *Über das Gedächnis: Untersuchungen zur experimentellen Psychologie.* Duncker und Humblot, Leipzig, 1885.

[FJZ05]   C. Früh, S. Jain, and A. Zakhor. Data processing algorithms for generating textured 3d building facade meshes from laser scans and camera images. *International Journal of Computer Vision,* 61(2):159–184, 2005.

[FL94]   O. Faugeras and S. Laveau. *3-D Scene Representation as a Collection of Images and Fundamental Matrices,* February 1994. Retrieved March 11, 2004, from ftp://ftp.inria.fr/INRIA/tech-reports/RR/RR-2205.ps.gz.

[Fla00]   D. Flanagan. *Java in a nutshell - Dt. Ausg. für Java 1.2 und 1.3.* O'Reilly, 3rd edition, 2000.

[Gar80]   P. Garner. *Möbel des 20. Jahrhunderts. Internationales Design vom Jugendstil bis zur Gegenwart.* Keyser, München, 1980.

[GMW02]   B. Goldlücke, M. Magnor, and B. Wilburn. Hardware-accelerated Dynamic Light Field Rendering. In G. Greiner, H. Niemann, T. Ertl, B. Girod, and H.-P. Seidel, editors, *Proceedings Vision, Modeling and Visualization VMV 2002*, pages 455–462, 2002.

[HBCN02] P. Hartling, A. Bierbaum, and C. Cruz-Neira. *Tweek: Merging 2D and 3D Interaction in Immersive Environments*. Iowa State University, 2002. Retrieved March 11, 2004, from http://www.vrjuggler. org/pub/Tweek_SCI2002.pdf.

[HTM03]   Z. Hendricks, J. Tangkuampien, and K. Malan. Virtual galleries: Is 3D better? In *Proceedings of the 2nd international conference on Computer graphics, virtual Reality, visualisation and interaction in Africa*, pages 17–24. ACM Press, 2003.

[ICO01]   ICOM. International Council Of Museums: Statutes with modifications adopted by the General Assembly in Barcelona on Friday 6th July 2001, 2001. Retrieved June 16, 2004, from http://icom.museum/statutes.html.

[Kal99]   K. Kaldenbach. Ein 3D-Flug über die 'Ansicht von Delft'; Johannes Vermeers Meisterwerk aus 1660 als virtuelle Welt. *Weltkunst*, 69(2):308–310, 1999.

[Kal00a] K. Kaldenbach. Expanding Vermeer's 1660 painting "The View of Delft" into a 3D Virtual Reality flight over Delft and a QuickTime "Walk Through Drawings of The View of Delft Area". In *Proceedings CIHA conference, London 2000*, 2000.

[Kal00b] K. Kaldenbach. Walking with Vermeer. Website, 2000. Retrieved November 2, 2003, from http://www2.io.tudelft.nl/ id-studiolab/vermeer/.

[Kar04]   C. Karp. Digitising Identity: The Museum Community Meets the Net. *DigiCULT - Thematic issue: Virtual Communities And Collaboration In The Heritage Sector*, (5):36–39, January 2004. Retrieved June 16, 2004, from http://www.digicult.info/ downloads/digicult_thematicissue5_january_2004.pdf.

[KHL+03] Y.-M. Kwon, J.-E. Hwang, T.-S. Lee, M.-J. Lee, J.-K. Suhl, and S.-W. Ryu. Toward the synchronized experiences between real and virtual museum. *APAN 2003 Conference, Fukuoka*, 2003.

[KWC00]   M. Kim, S. Wood, and L.-T. Cheok. Extensible MPEG-4 textual format (XMT). In *Proceedings of the 2000 ACM workshops on Multimedia*, pages 71–74. ACM Press, 2000.

[LH96]   M. Levoy and P. Hanrahan. Light Field Rendering. In *Proceedings of ACM SIGGRAPH 96*, pages 31–42, 1996.

[LJ80]   G. Lakoff and M. Johnson. *Metaphors We Live By*. University of Chicago Press, 1980.

[LJ99]   G. Lakoff and M. Johnson. *Philosophy in the Flesh: The Ebodied Mind and its Challenge to Western Thought*. University of Chicago Press, 1999.

[LM00]   F. Li and M. L. Maher. Representing virtual places - A design model for metaphorical design. ACADIA2000, 2000.

[Low99]   D. Lowe. Object Recognition from Local Scale-Invariant Features. In *International Conference on Computer Vision, Corfu, Greece*, pages 1150–1157, 1999.

[MA04]   P. Myers and D. Armitage. *Rattus norvegicus*. Last accessed 24 June 2006, http://animaldiversity.ummz.umich.edu/site/accounts/information/Rattus_norvegicus.html, 2004.

[Mal56]   A. Malraux. Museum without walls. *The Voices of Silence*, pages 13–127, 1956.

[Mie98]   G. Mietzel. *Wege in die Psychologie*. Klett-Cotta, 9th edition, 1998.

[Mie01a]   G. Mietzel. *Online Supplement zu "Wege in die Psychologie"*. http://www.supplement.de/supplement/index.htm, 2001.

[Mie01b]   G. Mietzel. *Pädagogische Psychologie des Lernens und Lehrens*. Hogrefe, Göttingen, 6th edition, 2001.

[Mus00a]   H.-P. Musahl. Stichwort "Experiment". In G. Wenninger, editor, *Lexikon der Psychologie (5 Bde.)*. Spektrum Akademischer Verlag, Heidelberg, 2000.

[Mus00b]   H.-P. Musahl. Stichwort "Versuchsaufbau". In G. Wenninger, editor, *Lexikon der Psychologie*. Spektrum Akademischer Verlag, Heidelberg, 2000.

[NB03]   K. Nowak and F. Biocca. The Effect of the Agency and Anthropomorphism on Users' Sense of Telepresence, Copresence, and Social Presence in Virtual Environments. *Presence*, 12(5):481–494, 2003.

[Nil99]   B. Nill. WWW-basierte interaktive Visualisierung der Rechenmaschine Wilhelm Schickards durch ein Java 3D-Applet. Seminar paper, 1999. Accessed April 27, 2005, from http://www.gris.uni-tuebingen.de/projects/studproj/schickard/index.html.

[NIS05]   NIST. National Institute of Standards and Technology - VRML plugin and browser detector, 2005. Retrieved May 2, 2005, from `http://cic.nist.gov/vrml/vbdetect.html`.

[Now04]   S. Nowozin. *Autopano-sift - Semiautomatic panorama generation using SIFT feature detection*, 2004. Retrieved March 11, 2004, from `http://user.cs.tu-berlin.de/~nowozin/autopano-sift/`.

[OCDD01]   B.M. Oh, M. Chen, J. Dorsey, and F. Durand. Image-based modeling and photo editing. In *Proceedings of the 28th annual conference on Computer graphics and interactive techniques*, pages 433–442. ACM Press, 2001.

[Pan05]   A. Pankov. Konzeption und Implementation eines Landmarken-Experiments zur Integration in Replicave. BSc thesis, University of Duisburg-Essen, 2005.

[PE02]   F. Pereira and T. Ebrahimi. *The MPEG-4 book*. Prentice Hall PTR, 2002.

[Pol99]   M. Pollefeys. *Self-calibration and metric 3D reconstruction from uncalibrated image sequences*. PhD thesis, ESAT-PSI, Katholieke Universiteit Leuven, 1999.

[Put94]   M.L. Puterman. *Markov decision processes*. Wiley, 1994.

[PWM+05]   P. Petridis, M. White, N. Mourkousis, F. Liarokapis, M. Sifniotis, A. Basu, and G. Gatzidis. Exploring and Interacting with Virtual Museums. In *Computer Applications and Quantitative Methods in Archaeology (CAA)*, March 2005.

[RR01]   G Rothfuss and C. Ried. *Content Management mit XML*. Springer, 2001.

[RT99]   W.B. Rayward and M.B. Twidale. From Docent to Cyberdocent: Education and Guidance in the Virtual Museum. *Archives and Museum Informatics*, (13):23–53, 1999.

[Sch04]   W. Schweibenz. The Development of Virtual Museums. *ICOM News*, 57(3), 2004.

[Sel02]   D. Selman. *Java 3D Programming*. Manning, Greenwich, 2002.

[Ski38]   B.F. Skinner. *The Behavior of Organisms: An Experimental Analysis*. Appleton Century Crofts, New York, 1938.

[Ski59]   B.F. Skinner. *Cumulative Record: Definitive Edition*. BF Skinner Foundation, Morgantown, 1959.

[Ski84]   B.F. Skinner. *The Shaping of a Behaviorist: Part Two of an Auto-biography.* University Press, New York, 1984.

[SM00]   S.D. Steck and H.A. Mallot. The role of global and local landmarks in virtual environment navigation. *Presence,* 9(1):69–83, 2000.

[SP05]   B. Shneiderman and C. Plaisant. *Designing the user interface.* Pearson Education, 4th edition, 2005.

[Spe60]   G. Sperling. The information available in brief visual presentations. *Psychological Monographs: General and Applied,* 74(11, Whole No. 498):1–29, 1960.

[Spe06]   G. Sperling. Personal webpage, `http://aris.ss.uci.edu/HIPLab/staff/sperling/sperling.html`, 2006.

[Sta00]   W. Stangl. *Internet @ Schule.* Studienverlag, Innsbruck, 2000.

[Süs03]   E. Süselbeck. Erstellung eines VRML-basierten Systems zum Gedächnisexperiment von Hermann Ebbinghaus als Schlüsselexperiment der Psychologie unter Berücksichtigung verschiedener Nutzergruppen. Master's thesis, University of Duisburg-Essen, 2003.

[SvG00]   J. Seemann and J. W. von Gudenberg. *Software-Entwurf mit UML.* Springer, 2000.

[SWN05]   D. Shreiner, M. Woo, and J. Neider. *OpenGL Programming Guide.* Addison Wesley, 5th edition, 2005.

[TB98]   O. Tchernichovski and Y. Benjamini. The dynamics of long-term exploration in the rat. Part II: An analytical model of the kinematic structure of rat exploratory behavior. *Biological Cybernetics,* 78(6):433–440, 1998.

[TBG98]   O. Tchernichovski, Y. Benjamini, and I. Golani. The dynamics of long-term exploration in the rat. Part I: A phase-plane analysis of the relationship between location and velocity. *Biological Cybernetics,* 78(6):423–432, 1998.

[TH30]   E.C. Tolman and C.H. Honzik. Introduction and removal of reward, and maze performance in rats. *University of California Publications in Psychology,* (4):257–275, 1930.

[Tra86]   W. Traxel. Hermann Ebbinghaus und die experimentelle Erforschung des Gedächnisses: Anmerkungen zu einem Jubiläum. In W. Traxel and H. Gundlach, editors, *Ebbinghaus-Studien 1: Arbeiten aus dem Institut,* pages 11–21. Passavia Universitätsverlag, 1986.

[UNE03]   UNESCO.   *Charter on the Preservation of the Digital Her-*
          itage.   http://portal.unesco.org/ci/en/ev.php-URL_ID=
          13366&URL_DO=DO_TOPIC&URL_SECTION=201.html, 2003.

[Vel02]   K.H. Veltman.   Digital Interpretation: To See the Un-
          seen History, April 2002.   Unpublished Keynote: Fronti-
          ers in Digital Interpretation.   Last accessed 30 June 2006,
          http://www.sumscorp.com/articles/pdf/2002%20Frontiers%
          20of%20Digital%20Interpretation.pdf.

[Wan02]   Q. Wang. VRML97 to X3D Translation. Technical report, Visualiz-
          ation and Usability Group in ILT, NIST, 2002. Retrieved March 11,
          2004, from http://ovrt.nist.gov/v2_x3d.html.

[Wat79]   F. Watson. *Die Geschichte der Möbel.* Südwest Verlag, München,
          1979.

[Wor04]   L. Wormuth.   *Schlüsselexperimente der Psychologie.*   2D project
          webpage. University of Duisburg-Essen, http://schluesselexp.
          uni-duisburg.de/tutorium/index_1.htm, 2004.

[Zid02]   V. Zidarich.   Virtual worlds as architectural space: An ex-
          ploration.   Technical report, FDL, 2002.   Retrieved March 11,
          2004, from http://www.fondation-langlois.org/e/activites/
          zidarich/zidarich.pdf.